Mentorship Mastery: Nurturing Growth and Success

How to be a Successful Mentor-Mentee

Gorilla Jones

Copyright

Dedication

This book is lovingly dedicated to my wife, whose unwavering support and belief in my journey have been the cornerstone of my endeavors. Her grace, patience, wisdom, and spirituality have been my constant source of inspiration and strength. To my mentors, who have generously shared their knowledge, experience, and time – this book is a testament to the invaluable lessons and guidance you have provided me. Your mentorship has not only shaped my professional path but has also enriched my personal growth in immeasurable ways.

And to those I have had the privilege of mentoring – your enthusiasm, curiosity, and dedication to growth have been a profound reminder of the transformative power of mentorship. Each of you has contributed to this journey in unique and meaningful ways, and it is my honor to have been a part of your stories.

Together, you all embody the spirit of "Mentorship Mastery: Nurturing Growth and Success." May this book be a reflection of the collective wisdom, encouragement, and shared journeys of growth and success.

Thank you for being my guiding stars.

Foreword

The landscape of personal and professional development is always evolving and changing. In response, mentorship can be viewed as a guiding light, illuminating the path to growth and success. Welcome to "Mentorship Mastery: Nurturing Growth & Success," where we embark on a transformative journey through the art and science of mentorship. In this first book, we lay the foundational stones upon which mentorship thrives, exploring its essence, principles, and the mindset that powers it. Together, we'll navigate the intricate web of mentor-mentee dynamics, forging bonds built on trust, empathy, and personal growth.

As you delve into these pages, you'll discover the critical importance of mentorship in today's dynamic world. Whether you're a seasoned mentor or a curious mentee, this book is your compass, guiding you towards unlocking the full potential of mentorship. We provide guidance, share stories, insights, and practical strategies to help you embrace mentorship's transformative power and cultivate an environment where mentorship flourishes. So, let us embark on this journey together and along the way you will soon see that mentorship is not just about nurturing others; it's about nurturing ourselves.

Contents

Introduction

A. Definition of Mentorship

Mentorship is the influence, guidance, direction, and elevation or boosting given by a mentor to the mentee. In an organizational setting, a mentor influences the personal and professional growth of a mentee. And the mentor often finds that the mentee influences them in the same way. Most traditional mentorships involve having senior employees mentor more junior employees, but mentors do not necessarily have to be more senior than the people they mentor.
You may even find that you are a mentor and a mentee at the same time – influencing, guiding, or giving direction to someone while you are being influenced, guided, and directed by someone else.

Mentoring may be internal, but it can also be external. An internal mentorship results when two people from the same organization invest time in a mentor/mentee relationship. The primary goal of internal mentorship is to enhance the mentee's professional development, help them navigate their career path within the organization, and contribute to the overall success of both the mentee and the organization. Internal mentorship fosters learning, knowledge sharing, and skill development while promoting a sense of belonging and a strong organizational culture.

In organizations where the availability of mentors with enough expertise in a particular area is exceeded by the number of those that should be mentored, that organization may seek external mentorship. External mentorship aligns a high-performance mentor from a different organization with a mentee in need. The goal of external mentorship is to provide guidance, share knowledge, and support the mentee in achieving their goals and advancing their career or personal development outside of their current organizational context. Often mentorship happens organically. In this environment the less experienced employee will ask for guidance in an unfamiliar situation. They are new to the organization or faced with a new project or problem. The more experienced employee will, through empathy or recognizing the need to keep things moving forward will offer guidance. Therein is the opportunity for developing a more formal mentor/mentee relationship where the other elements of successful mentorship discussed in this book can be brought to bear.

In companies where the win/win outcome of mentorship is valued, formal programs are found. Human Resources or management will provide direction to establish the mentor/mentee relationship using the elements of successful mentorship. A formal approach to mentorship can lead to high-level development for the mentee. For example, Cooley a global law firm, has a formal program called Cooley Academy Mentoring Program (CAMP)[1]. The program matches senior mentors with new hires to effectively and quickly onboard. Other examples include[2], Mastercard, Novartis, and McGraw Hill.

B. Importance of Mentorship in Personal and Professional Development

We will explore this a bit more in Chapter 1. Mentorship offers a transformative alliance between seasoned individuals and those navigating the intricate paths of growth, making it a cornerstone in the landscape of personal and professional development. In the realm of personal development, mentors serve as guides, imparting wisdom, and sharing experiences to help mentees navigate life's complexities. Through the lens of professional development, mentorship can be viewed as an agent for driving change and propelling individuals toward heightened success and fulfillment within their careers. The symbiotic relationship between mentors and mentees not only fosters the acquisition of valuable skills and knowledge but also cultivates a holistic understanding of self and one's professional aspirations.

At its essence, mentorship as discussed in this book delves into the realm of emotional intelligence, leadership, and self-discovery. Mentors, often possessing a wealth of experience, provide insight, steering mentees through the nuances of their chosen fields and career path. The reciprocal nature of mentorship, where both mentor and mentee contribute to a shared learning experience, underscores its dynamic and evolving nature. As mentors provide guidance, feedback, and support, mentees bring fresh perspectives, innovative ideas, and an eagerness to learn, creating a symbiosis that fuels not only individual growth but also the enrichment of the organization. In this interplay, mentorship becomes a conduit for the transfer of knowledge, the cultivation of resilience, and the forging of meaningful connections that transcend the boundaries of mere professional transactions. In the context of personal and professional development, mentorship emerges as an indispensable component of growth, empowerment, and the continual pursuit of excellence.

C. My Personal Experience and Journey with Mentorship

I am a senior quality assurance executive with over 35 years of experience helping pharmaceutical and medical device companies, so they are compliant with state, federal, and international regulations and provide direction for continuous improvement. Early in my career, I had the honor to be mentored by some exceptionally talented and knowledgeable people. In appreciation for their effort and later in my career I endeavored to return that mentoring gift to others. Whether a mentor or a mentee (sometimes at the same time) I found the experience profoundly rewarding.

I have often said that my first mentor provided directions on how NOT to do things. Shawn Branchard[3] would call this the "unconscious mentorship" phase of my mentoring experience. It was riddled with good examples, bad examples, and occasionally some bad examples. My first experience with mentoring was not formal, not planned, was not positively reinforced, was often my mentor's goals and not mine, and there was no considerable time investment in mentorship. As you will learn in this book all these elements are essential for a successful mentor/mentee relationship. But there were lessons to be learned and I wanted to learn. My mentor was a brilliant entrepreneur, skilled at teaching but not mentoring. I realized that as the mentee I had to take the initiative. I had to demonstrate my value, willingness, and worth to gain his commitment in the process.

As I adjusted my mindset about mentoring and learned from other mentors how the process should be done, I fell in love with the idea of being a mentor to others so the wisdom and knowledge gained through my hard work could be passed down to others ensuring that the next generation could develop the necessary skills, break free from the ordinary, develop self-confidence, have higher self-cognizance, and career progression. And most importantly, repeat the process at the appropriate time. I was also keenly aware that I could learn through mentorship. Mentees have so much to offer, and this should never be discounted.

Each chapter of this book ends with a "Call to Action" for mentors and mentees, allowing you to apply what you have learned. Let us move mentorship forward together by completing the "Call to Action" activities. As you immerse yourself in the principles and strategies of mentorship presented in this book, you can transform not only your own life but also the lives of those you guide. Turn that knowledge into action. So, act. Embrace Mentorship. Whether you are already a mentor or aspiring to be one, take the first step. Reach out to a potential mentee or seek a mentor who can guide you. Mentorship is a two-way street, and your journey begins with that first connection.

Please consider taking action to share your thoughts and experiences in mentorship. We welcome your real-world examples and will try to include them in our next book. While your experience is fresh on your mind, provide a review immediately on Amazon! I appreciate any feedback provided and it will be used to improve our book offerings for you and other readers.

D. Purpose and Scope of the Book

This book is intended to provide directions on how to be successful in mentorship and was written for those new to mentorship, those who have experience as a mentee but not a mentor, and those who are experienced as a mentor and a mentee. It is also intended to encourage the reader to become a mentor and mentee.

The term mentorship is used throughout this book and is intended to engage the mentor and the mentee. Considerable effort was made when authoring this book to engage both the mentor and mentee because mentorship is not successful without both being fully engaged in the mentorship relationship. When the term mentorship is used it is a call for the mentor and the mentee to apply the principles presented in their specific situation, keeping in mind that it is a mutually beneficial interaction. When done correctly, it is a win/win! I hope that this book will motivate you to get engaged in a mentorship.

This book is divided into five (5) chapters. Each chapter presents a key element to successful mentorship, breaks that element down into three or four sections that include strategies for implementation and concludes with a "List of High Points" from the chapter and a "Call to Action" for the mentor and the mentee. As additional guidance to help you be successful in mentorship real-world examples from mentors'/mentees' experience are included.

This book is not intended to be the definitive answer for mentorship. There are many valuable books, associations, and resources that explore mentorship, some of which are provided at the end of this book. So, whether you work in an organization that has a formal mentorship program, one that does not have a formal program, or you want to implement a formal program where you work, this book is an essential read. This book has a detailed table of contents that can be used as a reference for the reader who is looking for guidance in a particular element of mentorship. Simply use the table of contents to find the element of mentorship where you need support and go to that chapter/section.

Chapter One: The Foundations of Mentorship

A. Understanding the Mentor-Mentee Relationship

Mentorship is a dynamic and symbiotic relationship that goes beyond a simple transfer of knowledge. It is about the mentor's and mentee's personal and professional development. To comprehend the mentor-mentee relationship, it is essential to recognize it as a journey rather than a transaction. When viewed as a journey:

- **Focus on Growth:** Both the mentor and mentee prioritize personal and professional growth over short-term gains. They understand that mentorship is not about immediate results but about long-term development.
- **Investment in Learning:** Mentorship becomes a continuous learning process for both parties. It is not just about the mentor imparting knowledge but also about the mentee's active engagement in acquiring skills and insights.
- **Relationship Building:** The journey perspective emphasizes building a strong and trusting relationship. It is not a one-time interaction but an ongoing connection that deepens over time.
- **Adaptation and Flexibility:** Recognizing mentorship as a journey allows for adaptation and flexibility. Goals and objectives can evolve, and the mentor-mentee pair can adjust their course as needed.
- **Long-Term Impact:** Mentorship becomes a pathway for long-term impact, not just on the individual but on their career, personal development, and even the organization or community they belong to.

Embracing mentorship as a journey emphasizes the holistic and transformative nature of the relationship, where growth, learning, and personal development are at the core of the experience. It goes beyond a simple transaction of knowledge transfer and becomes a meaningful and fulfilling voyage for both mentor and mentee.

In this section, we will delve into the intricacies of this unique bond, exploring the mutual benefits, shared responsibilities, and the transformative power that stems from understanding and embracing the mentor-mentee relationship.

The Mutual Exchange

One of the fundamental aspects of mentorship is the interchange between the mentor and the mentee. Simon Sinek[4] suggests that it is a "mentor-mentor" relationship with each party to the relationship influencing, guiding, and directing the other. And why not? While the mentor brings experience, insights, and guidance, the mentee contributes fresh perspectives, energy, and a hunger for knowledge. Understanding and appreciating this exchange sets the stage for a meaningful and fulfilling mentorship journey.

All of you are in at least one friendship. Think of a friend. What do you do together? You are available for one another. You meet, share ideas, exchange information, and provide support. At times you are giving to that friendship and your friend is taking. Other times your friend is giving to you, and you are taking. You are both benefiting. I would even propose that you both give and take at the same time. There is a mutual exchange. Mentorship operates in very much the same way. When done properly, mentorship benefits the mentor and the mentee. Both need to be prepared to invest in mentorship to achieve this end. This is why it is so important to have a plan and to set aside time to execute the plan. Here are some benefits that can be expected by both the mentor and the mentee that we will show you how to achieve in this book:

- Feelings of personal accomplishment.
- Increased job satisfaction; increased employee retention.

- Stronger engagement in the work environment; steeper learning curve.
- Advance skills and professional growth; greater likelihood of promotion.
- Improved leadership abilities.

So, if the upside is so promising and mentorship is a win-win why do most people who value mentorship not have a mentor? Vinnie Malcolm[5] (Managing Partner at Malcolm Media Advisors) presented data suggesting that while 76% of people believe mentorship is important, only 37% of them have a mentor. Even when mentorship programs exist in a company some employees may be left to choose for themselves whether they want to participate in the available program. Assigning a mentor may not be a fix that will allow the successful mentorship relationship to flourish. Continue to read. There's work to be done! If your workplace does not offer a formal mentorship program, it might be time for you to implement one.

Shared Responsibilities

A successful mentorship involves shared responsibilities. Mentors guide, provide feedback, and share wisdom, but mentees also play an active role by seeking advice, applying lessons learned, and being receptive to constructive criticism. It is a collaborative effort where both parties contribute to the growth and development of each other.

Let us explore some of the responsibilities found in mentorship. What is provided here is not inclusive of all responsibilities. You will see as you read that mentorships are different from one to the other, much like friendships are not all the same. However, there are key responsibilities to all mentorship and some of those are presented here. Remember, these are shared and at some point, each party to the mentorship relationship will be taking on these responsibilities.

1. **Be genuine**: Each party to the mentorship MUST be someone who genuinely wants to see them succeed and

realize their potential. As a mentor, the direction you
will provide not only benefits the person receiving the
direction but the next generation as well. Because you
will provide direction with genuine sincerity the mentee
will reciprocate and will similarly share with someone
else. To demonstrate you are authentic in your approach
to mentorship, be prepared to use anecdotes from your
own experience throughout the journey.

Example:

Sarah, a young professional who had just started a new job
in a fast-paced tech company, was eager to excel and was
seeking guidance. Sarah was paired with James, an experienced and senior executive, as a mentor.

During their initial meeting, Sarah shared ambitions,
challenges, and aspirations openly and honestly. Sarah ad-
mitted to James that she often struggled with imposter
syndrome[6], feeling like she did not belong in the competi-
tive tech world. She also acknowledged that she was unsure about certain technical aspects of her role.

Rather than trying to impress her mentor or pretend to
know more than she did, Sarah displayed authenticity. She
expressed her desire to learn, grow, and overcome her inse-
curities. James, appreciating Sarah's authenticity, recognized her potential and assured her that it was entirely nor-
mal to face such challenges in a new role.

Sarah's willingness to be herself, share her vulnerabilities,
and seek guidance authentically contributed significantly
to her growth and development in her career. It also
strengthened her mentorship relationship with James,
emphasizing that authenticity is a powerful asset in
mentorship journeys.

2. Be enthusiastic: Go into mentorship with energy and
enthusiasm, making yourself available at all reasonable
times. Bring your passion to each interaction. Imagine you
are responsible for mentoring the next "most valuable em-

employee" at your company. Mentees share in the enthusiasm. You are about to embark on a transformative journey of personal and professional growth.

3. Endeavor to connect at the right level: Mentorship is not easy. You must be emotionally intelligent so you can interact in each situation with the proper sense of empathy and constructively work together through clear and concise communication and active listening. **Feedback is not always positive, but it should always be delivered positively**. Be empathetic. Call to mind your struggles and offer guidance using real-world examples.

4. Be willing to try innovative ideas or innovation: Be prepared to let your guard down and keep an open mind. Come with no pretense. You are going to share what you have learned and that may be turned on its head. Be willing to ask and respond to provoking questions. You will have to be open to being vulnerable to other people.

5. Accept diversity and inclusion practices: With experience should come a wealth of different perspectives. Be open to sharing that knowledge and learning new perspectives so you promote a culture of respect, belonging, and equal opportunity. Be a role model and inspire each other to emulate those same behaviors. You will see that the effect of your mentorship extends to the individual, the organization, and society.

Transformative Power

The mentor-mentee relationship has the power to transform individuals both personally and professionally. Through shared experiences, challenges, and successes, a mentor becomes more than a guide – they become a catalyst for personal and career evolution. Understanding this transformative potential is crucial for establishing a solid foundation in mentorship. The mentee becomes more than a receptacle for dumping information – they become an opportunity to nurture success, professionally and personally.

It will be repeated throughout this book, mentorship is a "two-way street." We must stop approaching mentorship with the mindset that knowledge flows in just one direction. Both parties should seek to learn and be guided by the other. If mentorship is approached from the standpoint that knowledge only flows in one direction, then both parties will not benefit from the time commitment required by mentorship, and one or both will feel unrewarded.

Research consistently shows that mentorship programs significantly impact leadership development. A study by Harvard Business Review[7] revealed that employees with mentors are five times more likely to get promoted and cites a five-year study of 1,000 employees by Gartner (2006) that found that 25% of employees who enrolled in a mentoring program had a salary change, compared to only 5% of workers who did not participate. Numbers like these underline the tangible benefits of mentorship, no matter your age or industry.

For those of you just starting your journey in the professional world and seeking mentorship you will have many questions from, "How do I find the right mentor?" to "What can I contribute to a mentorship with so little experience?" Early in the mentorship process, you may be receiving more than you are giving, that is okay, but you have much to share, and that will be revealed in this book and throughout the mentorship process. Never discount yourself. It is never too early to seek guidance.

Being new to mentorship you may be excited or feel nervous. That okay. Your mentor wants this to be a success for you. Keep in mind as you start this journey the following:

- You have so much to learn from your mentor. They can help you achieve your goals and overcome your challenges.
- You are making a positive choice for your personal and professional growth. You are also opening yourself to new opportunities and perspectives.

- You are not alone in this process. Your mentor is there to support you and guide you. You can also reach out to other mentees and peers for additional help and encouragement.
- You are doing a wonderful job as a mentee. You are building a trusting and respectful relationship with your mentor. You are also giving them feedback and appreciation for their time and effort.
- You are a role model and an inspiration for others. Being a mentee, you are demonstrating your commitment to lifelong learning and improvement. You are also setting an example for others who might want to seek a mentor in the future.
- You are learning and growing as a mentee. You are open to feedback and willing to try new things. You are also reflecting on your progress and achievements and celebrating your successes.
- You are a wonderful mentee. Enjoy the journey.

For those of you who are new to the role of being a mentor, remember that mentoring is a rewarding and fulfilling experience for both the mentor and the mentee. As a new mentor, you might feel nervous or unsure about how to best support your mentee. Here are some reminders to encourage you as you embark on this journey:

- You have so much to offer as a mentor. Your skills, knowledge, and experience are valuable and appreciated.
- You are making a positive difference in your mentee's life. Your guidance, encouragement, and feedback are helping them grow and achieve their goals.
- You are not alone in this process. There are many resources and support available for you as a mentor. You can also learn from other mentors and share your challenges and successes with them.
- You are doing a wonderful job as a mentor. You are building a trusting and respectful relationship with your mentee. You are listening to their needs and interests and adapting your style and approach accordingly.

- You are a role model and an inspiration for your
  mentee. They look up to you and admire you. They
  appreciate your honesty, integrity, and generosity.
- You are learning and growing as a mentor. You are
  open to feedback and willing to improve your skills.
  You are also gaining new insights and perspectives
  from your mentee.
- You are a wonderful mentor. Enjoy the journey.

For those of you in your 30s and 40s you may be asking
yourself, how can I refine my leadership skills, overcome
management challenges, or identify growth? You may be
seeking a balance of giving and receiving in mentorship. As
someone with a little bit of experience in mentoring, you have
already shown your passion, dedication, and generosity in
sharing your knowledge and skills with others. You are also
eager to learn from your mentees and improve your leadership
skills. Here are some reminders to encourage you as you
continue your mentorship journey:

- You have a lot to offer as a mentor/mentee. The
  experience, wisdom, and insight you have gained thus
  far in your career are valuable and appreciated. You are
  making a positive difference.
- Because of where you are in your career, you have
  demonstrated you are also a great learner and leader.
  You have learned how to receive and give feedback and
  are willing to challenge yourself. You are also
  respectful and supportive of your mentees' goals and
  interests. You are setting a good example for them and
  others.
- You are not alone in this mentorship journey. You have
  a network of mentors and peers who can support you
  and guide you. You are aware of various resources and
  tools to help you enhance your mentoring skills and
  leadership style.
- You have done a wonderful job as a mentor/mentee.
  You continue to build trust and meaningful
  relationships. You have progressed in active listening,
  encouragement, and empowerment. You continue to

grow in your mentorship skills and develop yourself as a leader and a professional.

- You are a role model and an inspiration. Those that you have mentored look up to you and admire you. They appreciate your honesty, integrity, and kindness. They also value your ongoing feedback, advice, and encouragement.
- You are finding a balance in giving and receiving in mentorship. You are generous and humble in sharing your knowledge and skills. You are also curious and grateful to learn from your mentors/mentees and others.
- You are an amazing mentor/mentee. Continue to enjoy the journey.

For those of you in your 50s and 60s mentorship does not go away. Make mentoring a lifelong journey of learning and sharing. Because of where you are in your career, you have a wealth of wisdom and insight to offer to others. You have mastered how to be open to innovative ideas and perspectives from your mentees and peers. Remain relevant while at the same time sharing your knowledge. It is never too late to seek and give guidance. Here are some reminders to encourage you to continue your mentorship journey:

- You are a treasure of knowledge and experience. Continue to generously share your expertise and guidance with others. You are making a positive impact on many lives and careers.
- You are a great mentor and a lifelong learner. You are always curious and willing to explore new possibilities and opportunities. You are also adaptable and flexible in changing times and situations.
- You are not alone on this journey. You have a community of mentors and mentees who appreciate and support you. You can also access various resources and platforms to help you stay connected and updated with the latest trends and developments.
- You are doing a wonderful job as a mentor. You are building strong and meaningful relationships with your mentees. You are listening to them, challenging them,

and inspiring them. You are also learning from them
and growing as a person and a professional.

- You are a role model and an inspiration for your
  mentees and others. They look up to you and respect
  you. They value your honesty, integrity, and generosity.
  They also benefit from your feedback, advice, and
  encouragement.
- You have found balance in giving and receiving. You
  are humble and grateful for sharing your knowledge
  and skills. You are also respectful and appreciative of
  learning from your mentees and others. You are
  creating a mutually beneficial and rewarding mentoring
  experience.
- You are an amazing mentor. Your time, effort, and
  commitment have a lasting impact on your mentees and
  the world.

"A mentor transforms lives. Find one to be one."[8] (Kristine
Zedek)

B. Key Principles of Effective Mentorship

Effective mentorship is rooted in a set of core values that
guide the relationship and ensure its positive impact on both
mentor and mentee. As we explore these principles, it
becomes evident that successful mentorship extends beyond
mere advice-giving. In this section, we look at commitment to
growth, open communication, and goal alignment.

Commitment to Growth

A commitment to the growth and development of the
mentee is a cornerstone of effective mentorship. Mentors
invest time, energy, and resources to nurture the potential of
their mentees, fostering an environment conducive to learning
and improvement.

Mentorship thrives on a shared commitment to growth.
Both mentor and mentee should approach the relationship with
a dedication to continuous improvement. This commitment

involves not only acquiring new skills and knowledge but also embracing a mindset that values curiosity and learning from every experience. By fostering a culture of growth, mentorship becomes a dynamic force propelling both individuals toward their full potential.

Here are some of the commitments you must be willing to make for successful growth through mentorship:

1. **Trust**: Trust is the foundation of any successful mentorship. Both mentor and mentee must trust each other's intentions and confidentiality. This can be achieved by fostering an open and honest environment where both parties feel comfortable sharing thoughts, concerns, and feedback.

2. **Respect**: Respect each other's perspectives, experiences, and boundaries. They may appear to be quite different at first but remember, be open-minded, and be patient. Begin by treating each other with dignity, listening actively, and acknowledging each party's unique strengths and challenges.

3. **Communication**: Clear and effective communication is vital for understanding and conveying expectations, goals, and feedback. Encourage open dialogue, provide constructive feedback, and ensure that both parties feel heard and understood. Going to stress patience here. Consider the possibility that one or both of you may not be "tuned in" to the planned mentoring session. You are just not into it at that time because of other distractions or commitments. Learn to recognize these often subtle traits. These are often excellent opportunities to mentor on something else. Perhaps use the session for something else that is taking precedence and get back with the plan during your next session.

4. **Empathy**: Understand and share the feelings of the mentee, demonstrating empathy in both personal and professional matters. Get them to speak on a personal

level. Be attentive to the mentees' challenges, offer support during challenging times, and celebrate their successes. Show respect by doing the same with them, calling to mind how you have been challenged comparably and how you overcame the challenge.

5. **Commitment**: Commitment involves a dedicated investment of time and effort from both the mentor and mentee. Set clear expectations regarding the time commitment, and consistently prioritize and schedule mentoring sessions. Avoid the challenges of time constraints as it may appear that you are not committed to the effort being made by the other person.

6. **Guidance, not Control**: Provide guidance and support, allowing the mentee to make their own decisions and learn from their experiences. Avoid imposing personal beliefs or decisions on the mentee; instead, facilitate their growth and decision-making process. Provide "real-world" examples from your experience and others. Be aware of mood when things do not go as planned.

7. **Professionalism**: Always maintain a professional demeanor, setting an example for the mentee in terms of behavior, ethics, and work standards. Remember why you got together. Never compromise your integrity or that of the other person. Uphold professional boundaries, avoid conflicts of interest, and adhere to ethical standards in both personal and professional interactions.

8. **Accessibility**: Be accessible and approachable, ensuring the mentee feels comfortable seeking guidance and support. Making yourself accessible is not losing control of your time or other commitments. It simply means organizing your time and communicating your availability. Provide regular and consistent communication channels, making it easy for the mentee to reach out when needed.

9. **Feedback and Growth**: Offer constructive feedback to aid the mentee's development, focusing on areas for improvement and recognizing achievements. **Feedback is not always positive, but it should always be delivered positively**. Establish a feedback loop, encourage a growth mindset, and help the mentee set and achieve realistic goals.

10. **Confidentiality**: Respect the confidentiality of information shared during mentoring sessions unless there is a risk of harm to themselves or others. Always adhere to the company's policy for confidentiality and restate, when necessary, the policy to the mentee ensuring there is no uncertainty. Create a safe space for the mentee to discuss sensitive issues without fear of judgment or breach of trust.

11. **Cultural Sensitivity**: Be aware and respectful of cultural differences, recognizing that diverse perspectives contribute to a richer mentoring relationship. Consider cultural nuances in communication styles, values, and expectations. The tone of voice, hand gestures, and body language may mean different things in diverse cultures. If you are uncertain or sense an issue, make a point of learning for both of you.

12. **Adaptability**: Be adaptable to changing circumstances and evolving needs within the mentoring relationship. Actively listen and use facial cues, body language, eye contact, and tone to stay in tune with changing circumstances and evolving needs. You will notice that one of you is unusually quiet or less prepared than usual. It may be necessary at those times to adjust mentoring strategies as needed, recognizing that each mentee is unique and may require different approaches.

By embodying these values, mentors/mentees can create a positive and empowering environment that supports their personal and professional development.

Open Communication

Effective mentorship hinges on open communication. Establishing a transparent dialogue allows for the free exchange of ideas, concerns, and feedback. Mentors/mentees should create a safe space to express thoughts and uncertainties. Simultaneously, mentors/mentees should actively communicate their goals, challenges, and expectations. Open communication forms the bedrock of a trusting relationship, enabling both parties to navigate the mentorship journey with clarity and mutual understanding.

Achieving open communication involves creating an environment where the parties to the mentorship feel comfortable expressing their thoughts, ideas, and concerns. It requires intentional efforts to foster trust, transparency, and active listening by both parties. Here are some strategies to achieve open communication:

1. **Lead by Example**: Mentorships should model open communication by being transparent, approachable, and willing to listen. When each member of the mentorship sees the other valuing open communication, they are more likely to follow suit.

2. **Establish Clear Communication Channels**: Define and communicate the various channels through which communication can take place, such as regular MS Teams meetings, one-on-one sessions, email, and collaboration platforms. The person taking the lead in the mentorship will ensure that each party to the mentorship knows how and when to use each channel.

3. **Encourage Questions and Feedback**: Create a culture that values questions and feedback. Encourage each other to ask questions, share opinions, and provide constructive feedback without fear of reprisal.

4. **Active Listening**: Actively listening to each other MUST be followed. This involves giving full attention, paraphrasing to confirm understanding, and asking clarifying questions. Active listening fosters understanding and demonstrates respect for others' perspectives. Mobile phones and other distractions should be turned off.

5. **Create a Safe Environment**: Establish a psychologically safe environment where both parties feel secure sharing their ideas and concerns. Provide feedback and celebrate learning opportunities and reaching milestones.

6. **Provide Regular Updates**: Keep one another informed about the mentorship's goals, strategies, and any changes. Regular updates help maintain transparency and ensure that each party is on the same page.

7. **Use Technology Wisely**: Leverage technology tools and platforms for communication, collaboration, and feedback. These tools can facilitate seamless communication, especially when face-to-face meetings are not possible.

8. **Implement an Open-Door Policy**: Those acting as the mentor should adopt an open-door policy, signaling their accessibility for discussions, updates, and feedback. This approach encourages the mentee to approach the mentor with their concerns or ideas.

9. **Make Mentorship More Than Just Meetings**: Agree to attend the other's activities such as presentations or training sessions to promote open communication. Allowing each party to the mentorship to see the other "in action" helps to build trust and strengthen interpersonal relationships.

10. **Celebrate Diversity**: Embrace and celebrate diversity between yourselves and within the organization. Recognize that diverse perspectives contribute to a richer pool of ideas and solutions. Encourage each other to share their unique viewpoints.

11. **Address Disagreements Constructively**: Seek amicable resolution to disagreements using conflict resolution skills and encourage the importance of addressing disagreements openly and constructively. Create a process for resolving disagreements while maintaining a positive mentorship environment.

12. **Set Expectations for Communication**: Communicate expectations for communication. This includes the frequency of updates, the use of specific communication channels, and the importance of timely responses.

13. **Regular Check-Ins**: Schedule regular check-ins to discuss progress, challenges, and goals. These meetings provide a structured opportunity for open communication.

14. **Seek and Value Input**: A big part of mentorship is to actively seek input, especially on important decisions. Demonstrating that the other member's opinions are valued encourages each person to participate more openly in discussions.

Remember that achieving open communication is an ongoing process that requires commitment and consistency. By implementing these strategies, you can create a mentorship culture where open communication is not just encouraged but becomes a natural and integral part of the journey.

Goal Alignment

Aligning mentorship goals with the aspirations of the mentee ensures a purposeful and impactful relationship. By understanding the mentee's objectives, mentors can tailor their guidance to address specific needs, making the mentorship journey more relevant and meaningful.

The mentor too should have clear objectives in the mentorship. Your approach as a mentor needs to be one of dedicating time, knowledge, resources, and experience to the mentee. However, do not short yourself either. Being a mentor is a wonderful time to sharpen leadership and communication skills. Consider where you need development and use the mentorship relationship to develop your leadership skills.

Example:
Mentorship: Laurene and Bethany's Story

Background:
Laurene, a seasoned Senior Document Manager with over 30 years of experience at Fountain Health Partners, a small medical device company, has recently taken on the role of mentor to Bethany, a new hire with little experience in document management in a regulated industry. Bethany's role as a Quality Assurance Administrator will involve supporting Laurene directly.

Development of Leadership Skills:

1. **Delegating Tasks**: Laurene identifies tasks that Bethany can handle, starting with simpler responsibilities and gradually increasing in complexity. This delegation process helps Laurene hone her ability to assess capability and readiness, a key leadership skill.

2. **Coaching and Feedback**: Laurene provides regular coaching to Bethany, guiding her through the company's procedures and regulations. She develops her feedback skills by offering constructive criticism in a way that is encouraging and leads to improvement, rather than discouragement.

3. **Problem-Solving and Decision-Making**: When faced
    with challenges, Laurene involves Bethany in the
    problem-solving process. She guides her through the
    decision-making process, enhancing her strategic
    thinking and leadership in mentoring Bethany to think
    critically.

4. **Team Integration**: Laurene takes the lead in
    integrating Bethany into the team, demonstrating
    inclusivity and team-building skills. She introduces
    Bethany to key team members and involves her in team
    meetings, highlighting her leadership in fostering a
    collaborative environment.

Development of Communication Skills:

1. **Effective Instruction:** Laurene develops clear, concise
    instructional methods to help Bethany understand
    complex document management systems. This process
    hones her ability to communicate complex ideas simply
    and effectively.

2. **Active Listening**: She practices active listening in her
    interactions with Bethany. By truly hearing and
    understanding Bethany's queries and concerns, Laurene
    improves her listening skills – a vital aspect of effective
    communication.

3. **Regular Check-ins**: Laurene establishes regular one-
    on-one meetings with Bethany. These sessions help
    Laurene practice and improve her verbal
    communication skills, ensuring clarity and
    understanding on both ends.

4. **Feedback Reception**: Laurene encourages Bethany to
    provide feedback on her mentoring style. This open
    communication policy allows Laurene to receive and
    process feedback effectively, an essential
    communication skill in leadership.

Outcome:

Through her mentorship of Bethany, Laurene significantly sharpens her leadership and communication skills. She has become more adept at delegating tasks, providing effective feedback, and making strategic decisions. Her communication skills, particularly in instruction, active listening, and feedback reception, are markedly enhanced. Bethany's successful assimilation into the team and her rapid skill development in document management are testaments to Laurene's evolved leadership and communication abilities. This mentorship journey not only benefits Bethany but also contributes significantly to Laurene's personal and professional growth.

C. Differentiating Between Mentorship and Coaching

While mentorship and coaching share similarities, they are distinct approaches to professional and personal development. Understanding these differences is essential for both mentors and mentees to navigate their roles effectively.

Mentorship vs. Coaching

Mentorship involves a comprehensive approach, encompassing not only skill development but also guiding broader aspects of personal and professional growth. It often draws from the mentor's experiences and insights.

Coaching, on the other hand, tends to be more task-oriented, focusing on specific skills and performance improvement. Coaches may not necessarily have direct experience in the mentee's field but are skilled in facilitating skill development.

See Figure 1 for a comparison of Mentorship and Coaching and where they overlap.

There is another title that you may encounter as you develop in mentorship. The term is "champion" or being someone's champion. I will not add a third term to this discussion, but it is important to understand that being a mentor or a champion is not the same thing, albeit there is some crossover as we saw with "coaching." Suffice it to say, that mentors offer guidance and advice, while champions actively advocate the success of the person they support.

The Synergy of Both Approaches

Recognizing the strengths of both mentorship and coaching allows mentors to provide a well-rounded guidance experience. By understanding when to adopt a mentoring or coaching stance, mentors can tailor their approach to meet the unique needs of their mentees.
While mentorship offers a broader perspective and guidance on overall growth, coaching provides targeted support for skill development and goal achievement.

Figure 1 – Comparison of Mentorship and Coaching

	Mentorship	Coaching	Overlap
Relationship Nature	- Long-term - More experienced person guides (mentors) & supports less experienced person	- Shorter-term - Task-specific relationship focused on enhancing specific skills; achieving goals	- Both provide feedback - Nature and context of feedback may differ
Scope & Depth	- Covers a broad range of topics - Mentor uses own experience to provide insights & advice	- More task oriented - Focused on specific skills or outcomes - Coaches address areas that need improvement	- Both aim to facilitate professional development
Personal Connection	- Involves a personal connection - Sharing of personal experience	- Emphasis is on skill development - Less used are personal experiences or anecdotes	- Both involve some level of rapport and trust-building
Goal	- Overall development & growth - Encompasses professional and personal	- Skill enhancement - Performance improvement - Defined Timeline	- Both tailor their guidance to the unique needs and goals of the individual
Example	Senior marketing exec serves as a mentor to a junior marketing employee providing guidance & direction on career advancement & navigating the complexities of the industry. They share insights gained from their own experiences while the mentee gains a broader perspective on their career.	An employee in a sales role engages a coach to improve their presentation skills. The coach conducts sessions focused on presentation skills. The coaching relationship is centered around achieving measurable improvements in the employee's presentation abilities.	

Figure 1 – Comparison of Mentorship and Coaching

Example:
Blending Mentorship and Coaching: Dick and Jane's Journey

Background:
Jane, an experienced marketing director, mentors Dick, a young marketing associate in the same company. Dick, ambitious and talented, aims to eventually lead his own marketing campaigns and take on a leadership role in the future. Jane's mentorship with Dick involves both mentoring and coaching to provide comprehensive guidance.

Phase 1: Mentorship for Career Guidance
1. **Career Path Discussions:** Jane starts by discussing Dick's long-term career aspirations, including his interest in leading marketing campaigns, and moving into a leadership role. She shares her career trajectory, offering insights into the skills and experiences required for advancement in their field.

2. **Networking and Industry Insight:** Jane introduces Dick to key contacts in the industry and includes him in high-level meetings to expand his network and industry understanding. She advises Dick on industry trends and the broader aspects of marketing that go beyond his current role.

Phase 2: Coaching for Skill Development
1. **Specific Skill Enhancement:** Identifying that Dick needs to improve his data analytics skills, which are crucial for campaign management, Jane shifts to a coaching stance. She sets specific, measurable goals for Dick to enhance his analytics skills and recommends courses and resources.

2. **Regular Check-ins and Feedback:** Jane schedules bi-weekly check-ins focused solely on Dick's progress in data analytics. During these sessions, she provides

focused feedback on his work, offering advice on how to interpret data more effectively.

Phase 3: Integrating Both Approaches
1. **Project Leadership Opportunity:** Jane assigns Dick a small-scale marketing campaign to lead. This presents an opportunity to apply his enhanced analytics skills (coaching aspect) and to develop leadership and strategic planning skills (mentorship aspect).

2. **Ongoing Support and Guidance:** Throughout the project, Jane provides continuous mentorship on strategic decision-making and client relations while coaching Dick on the tactical aspects of campaign management.

3. **Reflective Discussions:** Post-campaign, Jane and Dick engage in reflective discussions, a mentorship strategy, where they analyze both the successes and the learning opportunities from the project.

4. **Preparation for Future Roles:** In their mentorship discussions, Jane helps Dick envision and prepare for future roles, encouraging him to think about the kind of leader he wants to become and the broader impact he wishes to have in the marketing field.

Outcome:
Through this blended approach, Dick receives holistic guidance and develops specific marketing skills through coaching and gains broader career insights and professional development through mentorship. Jane's ability to alternate between being a mentor and a coach allows Alex to grow both tactically in his immediate role and strategically in his long-term career.

D. Why Mentorship is Needed in Today's World

In the rapidly evolving landscape of today's world, mentorship has become more than a traditional practice—it is a necessity for personal and professional success for both parties to the mentorship.

Mentorship is an essential aspect of personal and professional development. It is a relationship between a more experienced individual (mentor) and a less experienced individual (mentee) that is built on trust, respect, and mutual learning. Mentorship can provide numerous benefits for both mentors and mentees. Here are some ways in which mentorship can be beneficial:

Benefits to the mentee:
- **Guidance and advice**: Mentees can receive guidance and advice from their mentors, who have more advanced knowledge or experience in their field. This can help mentees grow and develop as professionals.
- **Increased confidence**: Mentees can gain confidence in their abilities through the support and encouragement of their mentors. This can help them take on new challenges and achieve their goals.
- **Personal or professional development opportunities**: Mentees can gain access to new opportunities for personal or professional development through their mentor's network and connections.
- **Awareness of other approaches**: Mentees can learn about different approaches to problem-solving and decision-making through their mentor's guidance and advice.
- **Opportunity to test innovative ideas and learn important processes**: Mentees can test innovative ideas and learn important processes under the guidance of their mentors. This can help them develop new skills and knowledge.

Benefits to the mentor:
- **Personal growth**: Mentors can experience personal growth through the process of mentoring. They can develop new skills, gain new perspectives, and learn from their mentees.
- **Professional development**: Mentors can gain new insights into their field through their mentees' experiences and perspectives. This can help them stay up to date with the latest trends and developments in their field.
- **Networking**: Mentors can expand their professional network through their mentees' connections and contacts.
- **Opportunity to give back**: Mentors can experience the satisfaction of giving back to their profession by helping others grow and develop.

In summary, mentorship is needed in today's world because it can provide numerous benefits for both mentors and mentees. It is a relationship built on trust, respect, and mutual learning that can help individuals grow and develop personally and professionally.

Accelerating Learning Curves

The pace of change in various industries requires individuals to adapt quickly. This can be true for the young employee as well as the more senior employee. When done properly, mentorship accelerates learning curves by providing both parties with insights gained through experience, helping them navigate challenges and seize opportunities with confidence.

Mentorship will provide guidance, support, and feedback to help both parties develop new skills and knowledge more quickly. Here are some ways in which mentorship can help:

1. **Experience**: Both parties have experiences that they bring to the mentorship. The person with more experience (often called the mentor) in their field can provide valuable insights into the industry. They can

help the person with less experience avoid common mistakes and pitfalls and provide guidance on how to navigate complex situations. The person with less experience can present ideas and ask questions of the person with more experience that challenge the status quo.

2. **Networking**: Both parties have some level of networking in a formal and informal sense. One party may have more contacts through social media networking while the other may have more private or secure networking contacts. Each can introduce the other to professionals in your field, expanding both networks and providing opportunities for growth and development.

3. **Accountability**: Both parties should hold the other accountable for meeting the mentorship goals established and help each other stay on track. Both can provide constructive feedback about the mentorship relationship and help each other to identify areas for improvement.

4. **Motivation**: Both parties in the mentorship will need to provide motivation and encouragement, helping both stay focused and committed to the mentorship goals. This is not always easy, especially when external forces are a distraction, or the mentorship has been long-running.

5. **Perspective**: Perspective is something that both parties can bring to the mentorship. The less experienced person can seek a fresh perspective on work, helping the other to see things from a different angle and identify new growth opportunities. The more experienced person can challenge the other by asking them to provide a fresh perspective on work through a younger more technology-driven perspective, for example.

Fostering Innovation and Collaboration

In a globalized and interconnected world, innovation and collaboration are key drivers of success. Mentorship promotes these qualities by fostering a culture of sharing ideas, experiences, and diverse perspectives, contributing to both individual and organizational growth.

Mentorship can foster innovation and collaboration in several ways. According to a Zinnov article[9] (a business consulting and service company, The Woodlands, Texas), mentorship is more of a collaboration than a skewed relationship presented previously. It is an approach to finding a unique way to solve the same problem by collaborating and anchoring on each party's experiences and expertise. The mentor can provide the mentee with valuable insights into the industry, help them avoid common mistakes and pitfalls, and provide guidance on how to navigate complex situations. They can also introduce mentees to other professionals in their field, expanding their network and providing opportunities for growth and development as mentioned above.

Through regular communication and collaboration with the mentor, the mentee can learn how to work effectively with others and build strong, cohesive teams. Overall, mentorship can be a valuable tool for fostering innovation and collaboration in various fields.

Navigating Career Ambiguity

Career paths are no longer linear, and ambiguity is constant, especially for the less experienced employee. Mentorship provides a guiding light, helping the less experienced navigate uncertain career terrain, make informed decisions, and build resilience in the face of change. It also helps the more experienced employees identify areas for improvement and develop onboarding and employee development programs.

Here's how mentorship can provide clarity and guidance:

1. **Clarifying Expectations**: The mentor can help the mentee understand their roles, responsibilities, and expectations. This includes clarifying job duties as defined within the written job description (if there is not one, there should be), performance expectations explaining how someone successful in the role would perform, and long-term career goals. The mentor can use this information to remove ambiguity.

2. **Navigating Organizational Culture**: The mentee may struggle to understand the unwritten rules and norms of the workplace, especially if this is a first job. The mentor can provide insights into the organizational culture, helping the mentee to navigate office dynamics and expectations. The mentor can then share with H/R the struggles identified to improve the onboarding process for all employees.

3. **Career Path Guidance**: The mentorship is going to include long-term planning. The mentor can assist the mentee in mapping out a career path. The mentor can share their own experiences, offer advice on skill development, and guide potential career trajectories within the organization. The career path should be developed through guidance and not handed to the mentee.

4. **Skill Development**: It is common for each member of the mentorship to identify skill gaps in the other. The mentor can help identify the skills and competencies needed for success in the role of the mentee. They can guide the mentee in developing these skills through training, learning opportunities, and on-the-job experiences. The mentee will identify gaps in the mentorship process helping the mentor to develop their mentoring skills.

5. **Building Confidence**: Mentorship includes encouragement and support of the other. The mentee will often face self-doubt and personal incompetence, sometimes referred to as "imposter syndrome." The mentor will encourage, share stories of their challenges, and offer support, helping the other build confidence in their abilities. When necessary, a "brag sheet" can be developed for the mentee as one way of reminding them of their successes.

6. **Problem-Solving Assistance**: All employees face challenges of varying degrees. When faced with ambiguous situations or challenges, the mentee can turn to their mentor for advice. The mentor can draw on their experiences to guide problem-solving and decision-making. The use of real-world examples is highly effective.

7. **Workplace Etiquette**: Although more of us can work from home than ever before, professional conduct is not only necessary but expected. The mentee may be unfamiliar with workplace etiquette, especially if visits to the office are not daily. The mentor can guide professional behavior, communication norms, and people skills, helping the other navigate the social aspects of the workplace.

8. **Stress Management**: Stress and coping with pressure are on the rise for a variety of reasons. Work-related stress and pressure can contribute to ambiguity. The mentor can share coping strategies, and stress management techniques, and help the mentee maintain a healthy work-life balance.

9. **Encouraging Questions**: A mentorship relationship should promote curiosity and encourage both members to ask questions and seek clarification without fear of judgment. This promotes a culture of open communication and reduces ambiguity about tasks or expectations.

10. **Facilitating Learning Opportunities**: Mentorship is about continuous learning. Both members should recommend learning opportunities, training programs, and resources to help each other stay updated on industry trends and technology and acquire new skills.

By providing guidance, support, and a safe environment for questions, mentorship helps the mentee gain a clearer understanding of their roles, navigate workplace challenges, and develop the skills needed for success. This, in turn, reduces ambiguity and uncertainty, contributing to their professional growth and confidence. The mentor gains helpful insights to improve mentorship skills as well as improve company-wide processes such as onboarding, training, and leadership development.

Closing the Generational Gap

With a multigenerational workforce, mentorship bridges the gap between seasoned professionals and emerging talent. It creates a platform for the transfer of knowledge, skills, and wisdom, ensuring a seamless transition of expertise across generations.

According to an AARP survey on multigenerational work and mentorship, mentorship can play a key role in promoting a positive attitude toward an age-diverse work environment[10]. The survey found that workers value the unique perspectives that a multigenerational workforce brings to their jobs. Seven in ten workers say they like working with generations other than their own, and the majority agree that both younger and older workers bring a set of positive benefits that enhance the workplace environment. Mentorship programs provide an excellent opportunity for knowledge sharing and fostering inter-generational understanding[11]. Mentors can provide mentees with valuable insights into the industry, help them avoid common mistakes and pitfalls, and provide guidance on how to navigate complex situations. They can also introduce mentees to other professionals in their field, expanding their network and providing opportunities for growth and development. Through regular communication and collaboration with mentors, mentees can learn how to work effectively with others and build strong, cohesive teams.

In conclusion, in Chapter 1 we learned that understanding the foundations of mentorship sets the stage for a meaningful and impactful journey. As we delve deeper into the subsequent chapters, we will explore how these principles can be applied in real-world scenarios, providing actionable insights for mentors and mentees alike.

List of Chapter 1 Highpoints:
- Mentorship is a dynamic and symbiotic relationship that goes beyond a simple transfer of knowledge.
- The mentor-mentee relationship has the power to transform individuals both personally and professionally.
- Effective mentorship is rooted in a set of core values that guide the relationship and ensure its positive impact on both mentor and mentee.
- Aligning mentorship goals with the aspirations of the mentee ensures a purposeful and impactful relationship.
- Mentorship is different than coaching.
- In the rapidly evolving landscape of today's world, mentorship has become more than a traditional practice—it is a necessity for personal and professional success for both parties to the mentorship.
- With a multigenerational workforce, mentorship bridges the gap between seasoned professionals and emerging talent.

Call to Action for the Mentor:
1. If your workplace does not offer a formal mentorship program, implement one.
2. Ask yourself: Would it be worthwhile to be a mentor?
3. Determine if you have the time and dedication to mentor.

4.   Document a list of goals and aspirations for mentorship.

Call to Action for the Mentee:
1.   If your workplace does not offer a formal mentorship program, implement one.
2.   Ask yourself: Would it be worthwhile to receive mentorship?
3.   Set aside time for personal reflection to determine your strengths, weaknesses, and goals.
4.   Document a list of goals and aspirations for mentorship.

Chapter Two: The Mentor's Mindset

A. Cultivating a Positive and Supportive Mentoring Mindset

When entering a mentorship, the mindset both parties bring to the relationship significantly influences its success and impact. In this section, we will present some ways to cultivate a positive and supportive mentorship mindset that will lay the foundation for a nurturing and constructive mentorship experience.

The Power of Positivity

Positivity is contagious and sets the tone for the mentorship journey. When both parties maintain an optimistic outlook, the mentor and mentee create an environment where both parties feel motivated, encouraged, and empowered. Incorporate the following practical strategies for fostering positivity. These must be practiced, but you will soon see how they contribute to the overall well-being and growth of the mentorship relationship.

Here are some examples of positivity that you can practice:

Empathy and Understanding: Each party to the mentorship should strive to understand each party's perspective, challenges, and aspirations. Consider incorporating these elements into the mentorship to convey empathy and understanding:

1. **Active Listening.** Eliminate distractions and focus on fully understanding thoughts, feelings, and concerns. Make eye contact. Refrain from interrupting while the other is speaking.

2. **Asking Open-ended Questions.** Questions should encourage others to share more about their experiences, thoughts, and challenges.

3. **Acknowledging and Validating Emotions.** Recognize and respect feelings.

4. **Put Yourself in Their Shoes.** Imagine yourself in the other person's situation. This will enhance empathy and understanding allowing you to provide more meaningful and relevant support.

5. **Share Personal Experiences.** Present the other relevant personal experiences to enhance communication, show vulnerability, and demonstrate that your challenges are real, regardless of experience or seniority.

6. **Cultural Sensitivity.** Cultural differences do exist, and each party needs to be aware of and respect those differences. Acknowledging the differences can be enlightening and will influence each party's mentorship experience and perspective.

7. **Non-verbal Cues.** You must be engaged so the subtle nuances of facial cues, body language, and tone of voice can be recognized. These cues can provide valuable insights into the emotional state and may direct the meeting in another way, even off the agenda.

8. **Provide Emotional Support.** When recognized as needed, emotional support should be provided. Sometimes, rather than specific advice, empathy and understanding may be needed. You will see through mentorship that remaining positive may require striking a balance between offering guidance and providing emotional reassurance.

9. **Be Patient and Non-judgmental.** You have committed to mentorship and that means setting aside time to

ensure mentorship success. Never rush and always work together to create an environment where expression without fear or criticism exists.

10. **Adapt Communication Style.** You may come from vastly divergent backgrounds and experiences. Be aware of these differences and acknowledge that one or both of you will have to adapt your communication style to meet the needs and preferences of the other. Being willing to do so demonstrates flexibility and a commitment to understanding and connecting with others.

11. **Follow-up and Check-in.** Regular check-ins should be planned but can also be spontaneous. Something unexpected occurred within the organization. A simple spontaneous check-in (as well as those that are planned) demonstrates an ongoing interest in the other's well-being while reinforcing an empathetic approach to the mentorship relationship.

12. **Encourage Self-reflection.** Encourage each other to engage in self-reflection by asking thought-provoking questions. Allow the other time to explore their thoughts and feelings more deeply. Write down your thoughts and feelings and include them in your discussion during your next meeting.

Example:
Empathy and Understanding in Mentorship: Simon and Andrew at the Bountiful Fish Packing Company

Background:

Simon, a seasoned manager at a fish packing company, takes on the role of mentor to Andrew, a new employee who recently joined the company's processing team. Andrew is enthusiastic but faces challenges adapting to the challenging environment.

Demonstrating Empathy and Understanding:

1. **Understanding Andrew's Perspective:** Simon begins by spending time on the processing floor with Andrew, observing his work, and understanding the specific challenges he faces, such as keeping up with the pace and mastering the technical aspects of the job.

2. **Sharing Experiences:** Simon shares his own early experiences when he started in the industry, including the difficulties he faced and how he overcame them. This helps Andrew feel understood and less isolated in his struggles.

3. **Acknowledging Aspirations:** Simon has a one-on-one conversation with Andrew to discuss his career aspirations. Andrew expresses a desire to eventually move into a quality control role. Simon acknowledges this goal and discusses a potential path to get there.

4. **Empathetic Feedback and Guidance:** When providing feedback, Simon is empathetic. He acknowledges Andrew's efforts and progress before offering constructive criticism. For instance, he compliments Andrew's diligence but suggests time management strategies to improve his pace.

5. **Addressing Challenges Together:** Simon and Andrew collaboratively develop strategies to address Andrew's challenges. For example, they devise a daily plan for Andrew to gradually increase his processing speed without compromising on quality.

6. **Regular Check-ins:** Simon establishes regular check-ins, providing Andrew with a platform to share his concerns and progress. Simon listens actively, showing genuine interest in Andrew's experiences.

7. **Supporting Professional Development:** To help Andrew advance towards his goal, Simon arranges for

him to spend time with the quality control team. This exposure provides Andrew with insight into the role he aspires to and demonstrates Simon's commitment to his mentee's growth.

8. **Celebrating Small Wins:** Simon recognizes and celebrates Andrew's small victories, like when he meets a processing quota or receives positive feedback from the quality control team. This boosts Andrew's morale and confidence.

Outcome:

Through empathetic listening and understanding, Simon helps Andrew navigate the initial challenges at the fish packing company. Andrew feels supported and valued, which not only improves his performance but also fosters his loyalty and commitment to the company. Simon, in turn, feels fulfilled seeing his mentee's growth and knowing that his empathetic approach has made a significant impact on Andrew's professional journey. This mentorship relationship strengthens the team dynamic and contributes positively to the company culture.

Here are some directions and tips you can include in your mentorship relationship to foster effective communication:

1. **Open Communication**: Positive and open communication is fundamental to a successful mentorship relationship.
   A. **Establish Clear Expectations**: At the start of the mentorship relationship set clear expectations for communication. Define the frequency and preferred methods of communication, ensuring both parties are comfortable with the arrangement. Eliminate technological challenges.
   B. **Create a Safe and Judgment-Free Space**: This is mentioned here and throughout the book. Work together to create a safe and non-

judgmental environment for communication. Both parties need to feel comfortable where sharing their thoughts, concerns, and challenges can occur without fear of criticism. Talk about what concerns you so you can avoid unwanted criticism.

C. **Use Positive Language**: At times you will find that "thinking before speaking" goes a long way in avoiding misunderstanding. The language used should always be positive and constructive. Frame the conversation positively to enhance understanding and receptivity. **Feedback is not always positive, but it should always be delivered positively**.

D. **Active Listening**: A big part of mentorship is listening. Both parties must listen attentively, ask clarifying questions, and reflect on what the other is saying before responding.

E. **Encourage Questions**: Questions should be prompted and welcome in a successful mentorship. Appreciate the curiosity of the other when questions are asked, as it shows their engagement and desire to learn. Questions are especially useful in determining the direction of the mentorship, often providing insight into where the mentorship may be falling short of expectations.

F. **Be Approachable**: Each party must make themselves available, be approachable, and be accessible. A reasonable open-door policy makes it easy for each party to reach out when needed. Share calendars and set times so availability is clearly defined.

G. **Regular Check-Ins**: At the onset of mentorship agree to check-ins to discuss progress, goals, and any challenges and when they will occur. This consistent communication helps maintain a connection between the parties and ensures that both parties are on the same page.

H. **Be Clear and Concise**: Communicate clearly and concisely. Avoiding ambiguity helps prevent misunderstandings and ensures that the guidance and feedback provided will be effective. This is especially true of electronic communication where the nuances of face-to-face communication are lost. Read twice before sending keeping in mind that while you may clearly understand your communication the audience is not you but another person. Be particularly aware of communication early in the mentorship.

I. **Use a Variety of Communication Channels**: There are a variety of communication channels used in mentorship. This is good and a variety of communication channels are encouraged such as in-person meetings, video calls, emails, or messaging platforms. The channels used will depend on the comfort level of each party in the mentorship. There will be different preferences, and adapting to these preferences enhances communication. Discuss the different channels at the onset of the mentorship and determine which will be used immediately and which may come later.

J. **Share Relevant Information**: Adopt an attitude of keeping the other person in the mentorship informed. Do not assume they are updated on all that may be happening with the company or your industry. Often it is a whirlwind. Share industry insights, networking opportunities, and resources that can contribute to each party's professional development.

K. **Feedback Delivery**: Teach mentors how to deliver feedback effectively. A positive mentorship is one where constructive feedback is provided in a supportive manner, focusing on specific behaviors, and offering guidance for improvement. Pull from your experience, both positive and negative.

L. **Encourage Two-Way Communication**: I have stated throughout this book that successful mentorship is beneficial for both parties. A win/win. Each party should actively contribute to the professional development of the other. Each party should contribute. While the mentorship may be led by the more experienced person, the less experienced person should seek ways to contribute to the mentorship. I have yet to meet someone who knows everything.

2. **Goal Setting**: Discussing goal setting in mentorship is exciting and should be a positive experience. It presents an opportunity for the creation of the mentorship pathway, the road you will follow during the mentorship. Each party should have ideas in mind and be prepared to build the pathway to mutual success. A positive mentor helps the mentee identify and work toward achievable goals, providing guidance, feedback, and support along the way.

3. **Constructive Feedback**: Highlight the art of giving constructive feedback. Positive mentors focus on providing feedback that is specific, actionable, and aimed at helping the mentee improve rather than criticizing.

4. **Cultivating Growth Mindset**: Explore the concept of a growth mindset. Encourage mentors to foster a belief in continuous learning and improvement, both for themselves and their mentees.

5. **Celebrating Successes**: Remind mentors to celebrate the achievements, no matter how small. Positive reinforcement enhances motivation and reinforces a sense of accomplishment.

6. **Encouraging Independence**: Emphasize the importance of empowering mentees to think

independently and make decisions. A positive mentor guides but also encourages autonomy.

7. **Adaptability**: Discuss the need for mentors to be adaptable. Different mentees may require different approaches, and a positive mentor is flexible in their mentoring style.

8. **Lifelong Learning**: Advocate for a commitment to lifelong learning. Positive mentors understand that learning is a two-way street, and they continually seek opportunities to enhance their knowledge and skills.

9. **Building Trust**: Stress the foundation of trust in mentorship. A positive mentoring mindset involves building a trusting relationship where mentees feel secure in seeking guidance and sharing their challenges.

10. **Role Modeling**: Highlight the importance of positive role modeling. Mentors can inspire by exemplifying the values and behaviors they encourage in their mentees.

11. **Patience and Persistence**: Remind mentors to be patient and persistent. Positive mentorship often requires time, and mentors should be committed to the long-term development of their mentees.

Supportive Mentoring: A Two-Way Street

Supportive mentorship is not only about providing guidance but also about actively listening to mentees' concerns, celebrating their successes, and being a reliable source of encouragement. In this section, we will delve into the many ways mentors can express support and create a collaborative and uplifting mentorship dynamic.

Supportive mentoring indeed thrives on reciprocity and collaboration. Here are some strategies mentors can use to express support and foster a collaborative and uplifting mentorship dynamic:

1. **Active Listening and Validation:** Practice active listening by giving undivided attention during discussions, reflecting on what is said, and acknowledging the mentee's feelings and perspectives. This shows respect and validates the mentee's experiences.

2. **Open-Ended Questions and Encouragement:** Ask open-ended questions that encourage mentees to think deeply and express themselves. This not only helps in understanding their viewpoint but also stimulates critical thinking and self-reflection.

3. **Sharing Personal Experiences and Vulnerabilities:** Share your own professional experiences, challenges, and even failures. This humanizes the mentor and creates a safe space for the mentee to share their struggles and learn from your experiences.

4. **Recognizing and Celebrating Achievements:** Acknowledge both big and small achievements of the mentee. Celebrating their successes boosts their confidence and reinforces positive behavior and effort.

5. **Providing Constructive Feedback:** Offer feedback that is constructive and aimed at helping the mentee grow. Balance critiques with positive reinforcement to ensure the mentee remains motivated.

6. **Encouraging Independence:** While providing guidance, also encourage the mentee to make their own decisions and solve problems independently. This fosters their growth and confidence.

7. **Setting Mutual Goals and Expectations:** Collaboratively set goals and expectations for the mentorship. This ensures both parties are aligned and have a clear understanding of the purpose and direction of the mentorship.

8. **Regular Check-ins and Adaptability:** Schedule regular check-ins to discuss progress, challenges, and any adjustments needed in the mentorship approach. Being adaptable to the mentee's evolving needs is crucial.

9. **Resource Sharing:** Provide resources such as articles, books, and courses, or connect the mentee with other professionals. These resources can offer additional perspectives and learning opportunities.

10. **Creating a Supportive Network:** Introduce the mentee to your professional network. Networking opportunities can significantly enhance their professional development.

11. **Empathy and Understanding:** Show empathy and strive to understand the mentee's background, challenges, and aspirations. This understanding is key to providing relevant and personalized support.

12. **Encouraging Professional Development:** Encourage and support the mentee in pursuing professional development opportunities, whether it is attending workshops, seminars, or pursuing further education.

By employing these strategies, mentors can create a nurturing, supportive, and empowering environment, fostering a dynamic where both mentor and mentee feel valued, respected, and motivated to grow together.

B. Developing Empathy and Emotional Intelligence

Empathy and emotional intelligence are fundamental to effective mentorship. Understanding and connecting with the emotions of your mentee enhances the quality of guidance and strengthens the mentor-mentee relationship.

Empathy in Mentorship

Empathy is the ability to understand and share the feelings of another. In mentorship, empathy involves putting yourself in the mentee's shoes, understanding their perspectives, and acknowledging their emotions. Mentors must grasp the mentee's perspective and emotions. We will explore how empathetic listening and responses contribute to a supportive mentorship environment, fostering trust and rapport.

Empathetic listening involves listening to the person speaking in the mentorship and then making an emotional connection and understanding their feelings. To do so effectively one must be attentive and responsive during conversations and not deny or dismiss the other party's concerns or challenges.

Do not overload your mentorship meeting agendas. If you are not familiar or comfortable with empathetic listening, you may have to deliberately slow the pace of your meetings down until you are more familiar and comfortable. You will have to take in not only what the other person is saying but what they are not saying.

Here are some of the skills you can practice becoming more successful with empathetic listening:

1. **No Judgment**: People often say, "Don't judge me!" In mentorship, both parties must strive to set aside their personal views and opinions. This can be done by focusing on the other person when they are speaking, accepting what they are saying, and showing that you are receiving and accepting the message. Be patient. There will be time later to make sure there are no misunderstandings.

2. **No Distractions**: Put that mobile phone aside and close your laptop. You must give your full attention without the possibility of interruptions to the other party when they are speaking.

3. **Not Just Words**: Giving your full attention to the other party when they are speaking means that you will also be aware of non-verbal communication such as facial cues, body language, and tone of voice. This will help you to consider what is behind the words and acknowledge the feelings being communicated by the other party. Head down, shifting away, arms folded across the body, and inability to maintain eye contact could signal that they are holding something back, they are not engaged in the mentorship meeting, or they feel uncomfortable.

4. **No Interruptions**: Silence is okay. Not every moment during mentorship needs to be filled with someone's voice. Pauses can be constructive time, allowing the speaker to put together their thoughts and to continue to speak once they are ready. Encouragement such as "take your time" is helpful. For the listener, this is an opportunity to refocus their attention on the speaker, maintain eye contact, and use nonverbal cues such as nodding or smiling to show that you are engaged.

5. **No Misunderstandings:** When the other party has finished speaking, always make sure to summarize and clarify your understanding of what they just shared. This includes an emotional message. Putting a label on an emotion is helpful to the speaker, especially if they have a challenge to do so. Avoid defensive language, direct questions, and disputing facts. These concerns can be addressed later. Concentrate on what is being said and how the other party feels.

6. **No Sitting Still**: Active listening is a part of empathetic listening. While listening to the other party speak demonstrate that you are listening by sitting attentively (no slouching), smiling, and nodding your head. Simple acknowledgments such as these are not disruptive to the speaker but the feedback, they receive will go a long way in encouraging open communication and trust. It should be understood by the parties that nodding and

smiling are not an indication of agreement, but rather acknowledgment of what is being said.

Here are a few suggestions for both parties to the mentorship that will allow you to practice empathetic listening:

1. **Practice Being Silent**: Agree at the start of a mentorship meeting that one party will intentionally pause while speaking and the other will maintain eye contact, smile, and just wait in silence until the speaker continues. Switch roles. Reserve time in the meeting to provide feedback including what feelings each party experienced.

2. **Practice Non-verbal Communication**: Agree that while speaking, one party to the mentorship will use a variety of non-verbal cues. The listener will keep a list of comments on each as to what they were being told by the non-verbal cues. Discuss the non-verbal cues identified by the listener. Switch roles. Provide feedback.

3. **Practice in Unfamiliar Place**: One element of empathetic listening is "No Distractions." The goal of this exercise is to compel each party to speak and listen while trying to give their full attention and focus to the other party. Find a place that has distractions such as noise and foot traffic that are not usually encountered during a mentorship meeting. A restaurant, company dining area, or a park. Conduct your mentorship meeting to try to apply the skills listed above. Then, discuss your challenges and the tools you used to focus on the speaker.

There are many options online to practice empathetic and active listening. Explore your options and select one as a fun activity for the mentorship meeting. Do not forget to include feedback to each other.

Emotional Intelligence as a Mentor

Emotional intelligence involves recognizing and managing one's own emotions and understanding and influencing the emotions of others. Emotional intelligence enables mentors to navigate the complexities of the mentorship relationship with sensitivity and self-awareness. Mentors with high emotional intelligence can navigate the complexities of mentorship with greater effectiveness. They are attuned to both their own emotions and the emotions of their mentees. There are numerous online tests to determine your emotional intelligence.

In this section, we will discuss the key components of emotional intelligence and how mentors can enhance their emotional intelligence through empathy-building exercises, such as role-playing scenarios or reflecting on past experiences to better connect with and guide their mentees. In the context of mentorship, emotional intelligence (EI) refers to the mentor's ability to understand, manage, and effectively express their own emotions, as well as to interpret and respond appropriately to the emotions of their mentee. Emotional intelligence (EI) is a critical skill for mentors, enabling them to navigate the complexities and dynamics of mentorship relationships with sensitivity, understanding, and self-awareness.

Key components of emotional intelligence include:

1. **Self-Awareness:** Recognizing and understanding one's own emotions and how they affect thoughts and behavior. Self-aware mentors are better equipped to understand their reactions and the impact they have on the mentorship relationship.

2. **Self-Regulation:** The ability to control or redirect disruptive emotions and impulses. It involves being able to think before reacting, managing emotional responses to situations, and demonstrating reliability and integrity.

3. **Motivation:** Being driven to achieve for the sake of achievement, not just external rewards. This includes having a strong inner drive, being optimistic even in the face of failure, and being committed to personal and professional goals.

4. **Empathy:** The ability to understand and share the feelings of others. In mentorship, empathy involves being attuned to the mentee's feelings and perspectives and considering these in communication and guidance.

5. **Social Skills:** Proficiency in managing relationships and building networks. For mentors, this includes being excellent communicators, adept at managing conflict, and skilled at building and maintaining rapport.

6. **Active Listening:** Going beyond hearing what is said to understanding the underlying message. This includes paying attention to nonverbal cues and responding in a way that shows comprehension and consideration.

7. **Constructive Feedback:** Delivering feedback in a way that is helpful and not hurtful, focusing on the behavior rather than the person, and motivating change or improvement.

8. **Conflict Resolution:** Being able to navigate disagreements or misunderstandings in a way that is productive and does not escalate tension. This requires understanding different perspectives and finding common ground or solutions.

9. **Adaptability:** The ability to be flexible and adapt one's approach based on the situation and the needs of the mentee. It involves being open to innovative ideas and changes in plans.

10. **Compassion and Support:** Showing genuine concern for the mentee's well-being and offering support,

encouragement, and guidance in a way that is nurturing and empowering.

Emotional intelligence is integral to effective mentorship, as it helps mentors connect with their mentees on a deeper level, foster a positive and productive learning environment, and navigate the emotional aspects of the mentorship journey with grace and effectiveness.

Developing empathy is crucial for mentors to connect deeply with their mentees and guide them effectively. Here are some empathy-building exercises that mentors can use:

1. **Active Listening Practice:** Engage in exercises where the mentor listens attentively to the mentee without interrupting. After listening, the mentor should summarize what they heard to ensure understanding. This practice encourages deeper listening and understanding of the mentee's perspective.

2. **Role Reversal:** Temporarily switch roles, where the mentor plays the role of the mentee and vice versa. This exercise helps the mentor see things from the mentee's perspective, fostering greater empathy.

3. **Reflective Journaling:** Encourage mentors to keep a reflective journal about their mentorship experiences. Reflecting on interactions with the mentees and how they felt during those interactions can enhance self-awareness and empathy.

4. **Empathy Mapping:** Create an empathy map for the mentee. This involves noting what the mentee might be thinking, feeling, seeing, and doing in their role or life. This exercise helps mentors to better understand the mentee's experiences and challenges.

5. **Sharing Personal Stories:** Allocate time for both mentor and mentee to share personal stories related to challenges, successes, or failures. This mutual sharing

can build empathy and strengthen the mentor-mentee
bond.

6. **Perspective-Taking Scenarios:** Discuss hypothetical
   scenarios or past experiences and explore them from
   different perspectives. This exercise encourages the
   mentor to think about situations from the mentee's
   point of view.

7. **Emotional Awareness Exercises:** Practice identifying
   and articulating emotions during conversations. This
   could involve the mentor describing how they think the
   mentee feels about certain situations and then getting
   feedback from the mentee.

8. **Cultural Competence Learning:** If the mentor and
   mentee come from diverse cultural backgrounds, it is
   helpful for the mentor to learn about the mentee's
   culture. Understanding cultural influences can
   significantly enhance empathy.

9. **Feedback Sessions:** Regular feedback sessions where
   the mentee provides input on the mentorship style can
   be illuminating. It helps the mentor understand the
   impact of their actions and words on the mentee.

10. **Empathy in Action:** Actively encourage the mentor to
    respond to the mentee's needs thoughtfully. For
    example, if a mentee is struggling with a particular
    challenge, the mentor could offer specific support
    tailored to that challenge.

These exercises can help mentors develop and enhance
their empathy, which is vital for understanding and effectively
guiding their mentees. Empathy strengthens the mentor-
mentee relationship and creates a more supportive and
productive environment.

C. Recognizing and Overcoming Bias in Mentorship

Bias, whether conscious or unconscious, can influence mentorship dynamics and outcomes. Recognizing and actively addressing bias is essential for fostering an inclusive and equitable mentorship experience.

Unpacking Bias in Mentorship

Bias refers to preconceived notions or prejudices that influence judgment. In mentorship, bias can affect the mentor's perception of the mentee's capabilities and potential. Similarly, bias can affect the mentee's perception of the mentor's interest and willingness to be fully engaged in the mentorship.

There are several types of bias, and we will not go into great detail in this book. We will explore different forms of bias, such as gender bias, cultural bias, and affinity bias, and their potential impact on mentorship. Recognizing these biases is the first step toward creating a mentorship relationship that is fair, unbiased, and open to diverse perspectives.

Bias types include but are not limited to the following:

1. **Implicit Bias**: These are subconscious attitudes that influence decisions. It may not be intentional, but it can still have significant effects on decision-making. Implicit biases can influence perceptions, judgments, and behaviors, impacting various aspects of life, including interactions in the workplace. These biases can be activated automatically in various situations.

2. **Affinity Bias**: Preference is given to individuals with the same or similar background or experience. Sometimes referred to as similarity bias or in-group bias. This bias is rooted in a natural inclination to feel more comfortable and trusting towards people who are

perceived as part of one's own social, cultural, or professional group.

3. **Confirmation Bias**: Giving more weight to information that confirms existing beliefs. This bias refers to the tendency of individuals to favor, interpret, and remember information in a way that confirms their preexisting beliefs or hypotheses.

4. **Gender Bias**: Refers to the unfair and unequal treatment of individuals based on their gender, often favoring one gender over the other. Gender bias typically arises from preconceived stereotypes, cultural norms, and societal expectations associated with masculinity and femininity.

5. **Cultural Bias**: Refers to the presence of preconceived notions, preferences, or prejudices that favor certain cultures or cultural groups over others. Your mentorship can work towards creating environments that value and respect diverse cultural perspectives. Lead by example through your mentorship.

Detecting Signs of Bias in Mentorship

Bias can manifest itself in several diverse ways. It may be unknown to the person who is demonstrating bias so awareness will be the first step in overcoming bias. Other strategies are discussed below. When bias is detected the goal of the mentor/mentee should be to minimize or eliminate the bias. Understanding and addressing bias is essential for fostering successful mentorship and a fair and just society.

Here are some ways that bias may be detected in the mentorship relationship through communication and actions:

1. **Stereotyping**: Assumptions made about certain characteristics or abilities based on an individual's gender. For example, assuming that women are more nurturing or that men are more assertive.

2. **Discrimination**: Individuals are treated unfairly or denied opportunities. This discrimination can occur in hiring processes, promotions, educational opportunities, and more.

3. **Inequality**: The creation of disparities in various aspects of life, such as wages, access to education, representation in leadership roles, and participation in certain activities.

4. **Microaggressions**: Subtle, often unintentional, verbal, or non-verbal expressions of prejudice. These can include comments or behaviors that reinforce bias.

5. **Intersectionality**: The intersection of other forms of bias, such as race, ethnicity, sexual orientation, or socioeconomic status. Intersectionality recognizes that individuals may experience multiple layers of discrimination.

6. **Cultural Influence**: Cultural norms and expectations bias. Societal beliefs about traditional gender roles may influence how individuals are treated and what opportunities are available to them.

7. **Impact on Mental Health**: Experiencing the effects of bias can hurt mental health. It may contribute to stress, anxiety, and a sense of not being valued or recognized for one's abilities and contributions.

8. **Language and Communication**: Communication styles may influence how language and communication styles are perceived. Diverse cultures may have distinct communication norms, and biases can emerge when one set of norms is deemed superior or more acceptable.

9. **Impact on Inclusivity**: Biases can contribute to creating non-inclusive environments, affecting diversity and equity. Be aware of such behaviors within and

external to the mentorship relationship making the other in the mentorship aware so it can be properly addressed.

10. **Exclusion**: Unintentional exclusion of those who do not share similar characteristics to one's group. Noticeable when there are cliques and homogeneous groups. Can impact collaboration and communication between individuals from diverse cultural backgrounds.

11. **Polarization of Views**: Existing perspectives may not be subject to challenge or opposing views. Sometimes seen when there is a desire to prevent the discomfort that arises when there are conflicting beliefs within a mentorship or group. In these situations, individuals may selectively seek out or emphasize evidence that supports their position, hindering open and objective dialogue.

Strategies for Overcoming Bias

In this section mentors/mentees will gain insights into practical strategies for overcoming bias, including self-reflection, education, and creating awareness within the mentorship relationship. By actively addressing bias, mentors contribute to a more inclusive and enriching mentorship experience for their mentees.

1. **Self-reflection**: The first step in confronting bias in mentorship is acknowledging the existence of bias. This can be accomplished through self-awareness. Each party to the mentorship needs to recognize their own biases before they can address them. You have biases. Reflect on what they may be and how they may impact the mentorship relationship. What can you do to overcome those biases?

Consider seeking a diverse mentor/mentee to challenge your biases. Exposure to different perspectives fosters a more inclusive and open-minded mentorship. Mentors/mentees should engage in regular self-reflection, examining their decisions and actions for signs of bias. This ongoing self-assessment contributes to a more equitable mentorship dynamic.

2. Education: Corporate education programs should incorporate training on recognizing and addressing bias. This could include workshops, seminars, or ongoing education to sensitize mentors/mentees to the impact of bias.

3. Promote Diversity and Inclusion: Actively seek and promote diverse representation in all areas, including hiring, leadership roles, and decision-making bodies. A diverse group brings a variety of perspectives that can counteract bias.

4. Encourage Open Dialogue: Create an environment, not just in the mentorship relationship, although this is a good place to start if a formal education program does not exist in your company, where open dialogue about biases is encouraged. Establishing communication channels allows individuals to express concerns, ask questions, and seek clarification.

5. Foster Inclusive Mentorship: Set the example your-selves through mentorship. Mentors/mentees play a crucial role in setting the tone for an inclusive environment-ment. Act as leaders who demonstrate inclusive behaviors and challenge bias to contribute to a positive organiza-tional culture.

6. Encourage Two-way Feedback: Establish mechanisms in your approach to mentorship to provide feedback on po-tential bias in processes or decisions outside of the mentor-ship relationship. Act on this feedback through the appro-priate channels to make continuous improvements within your organization.

D. Balancing Guidance and Autonomy

One of the delicate balances mentors must strike and mentees must accept is guiding while allowing room for mentees to exercise autonomy and make their own decisions. Achieving this balance is crucial for empowering mentees and fostering independence. Each party, through discussion, will have to understand their role. Open communication about expectations is key. Define the mentorship goals, the level of guidance the mentee desires, and the degree of autonomy they should have.

Guiding Without Dictating

Mentors will guide without imposing their preferences or decisions onto the mentee. This approach promotes critical thinking and decision-making skills, enabling mentees to become more self-reliant in their professional journeys. Mentors should aim to empower mentees to think critically and make informed decisions. This involves guiding them through problem-solving rather than providing all the answers. One approach is to adopt a phased approach to mentorship. Initially, mentors might offer more guidance, gradually allowing mentees to take on more responsibility as their skills and confidence grow.

Example:
Non-Imposing Guidance in Mentorship: Phillip and Bartholemew at a Fast-Food Chain

Background:
Phillip, a manager at a fast-food chain, is mentoring Bartholemew, an employee being groomed for the role of assistant manager for the night shift. The restaurant has recently experienced several thefts during the evening hours and Phillip wants to ensure Bartholemew is prepared to handle such situations effectively.

Phillip's Approach to Guiding Bartholemew:

1. **Situation Analysis:** Phillip begins by discussing the recent thefts with Bartholemew. Instead of directly telling Bartholemew what to do, Phillip asks open-ended questions like, "How do you think we can improve our security during the night shift?" This encourages Bartholemew to analyze the situation and think critically about potential solutions.

2. **Sharing Experiences, Not Dictating Actions:** Phillip shares his own experiences with handling similar situations, emphasizing the strategies he found useful. He says, "In my experience, staying vigilant and having a clear protocol helped me a lot. How do you feel about these approaches?" This way, he is offering insight without imposing his methods directly.

3. **Collaborative Problem-Solving:** Together, they review the current security measures in place. Phillip guides the discussion but allows Bartholemew to take the lead in suggesting improvements or changes. This collaborative approach empowers Bartholemew to take ownership of the problem and its solution.

4. **Encouraging Initiative and Independence:** Phillip encourages Bartholemew to produce his own set of actions to increase vigilance during the night shift. He says, "I trust your judgment. Let's hear what you think would work best in managing this issue."

5. **Providing Constructive Feedback:** When Bartholemew proposes a plan, Phillip listens attentively and then provides constructive feedback. He highlights the strengths of Bartholemew's plan and gently suggests areas for consideration or improvement.

6. **Support and Availability:** Phillip assures Bartholemew of his support and availability for

guidance, saying, "I am here to support you. Feel free to run your ideas by me anytime."

7. **Building Confidence:** Throughout the mentorship, Phillip focuses on building Bartholemew's confidence. He acknowledges Bartholemew's efforts and progress, saying, "Your approach to handling the security issue shows great initiative and leadership."

Outcome:

As a result of Phillip's non-imposing yet supportive mentoring style, Bartholemew develops the skills and confidence necessary to be an effective assistant manager. He learns to approach challenges independently but with the knowledge that he has a supportive mentor to guide him. Bartholemew implements a successful security strategy for the night shift, reflecting his growth under Phillip's mentorship. This approach not only solves the immediate issue of thefts but also prepares Bartholemew for future leadership roles.

Nurturing Autonomy

In this section, we provide a few specific strategies and insights for use in mentorship to foster autonomy successfully and how it contributes to their personal and professional development. Mentors must recognize and value the importance of mentee independence. This is a goal of mentorship. A successful mentorship involves preparing mentees to navigate challenges autonomously, contributing to their long-term success. Mentors will gain insights into fostering an environment that encourages mentees to take initiative, learn from mistakes, and become confident and capable professionals.

Effective mentors tailor their approach to the individual needs of each mentee. Since each person is unique, so should the mentor's approach to mentorship. Some mentees may thrive with more guidance, while others may prefer a more hands-off approach. As part of your regular check-ins, each party should assess their comfort level with the mentoring dynamic. Seek feedback on the balance between guidance and autonomy and adjust as needed.

As the mentee moves to greater autonomy these milestones should be celebrated. Recognition reinforces the mentee's sense of accomplishment and encourages continued growth. In the same way, recognition validates the mentor's approach to mentorship and motivates them to future success with other mentees.

Following are some strategies for nurturing autonomy:

1. **Set Clear Expectations**: Communicate the expectations for autonomy within the mentorship. Discuss the level of independence the mentee desires and establish boundaries for guidance.
2. **Offer Guidance, Not Answers**: Instead of providing direct answers, guide mentees through problem-solving processes. This approach helps them develop critical thinking skills and autonomy.
3. **Provide Resources and Empowerment Tools**: Equip mentees with the necessary resources and tools to navigate challenges on their own. This includes knowledge, skills, and access to relevant networks.
4. **Provide Challenges**: Offer mentees challenges that push their boundaries. This not only encourages autonomy but also stimulates continuous learning and skill development.
5. **Promote Decision-Making**: Encourage mentees to take ownership of their decisions. Discuss the reasoning behind choices rather than dictating solutions, allowing them to understand the decision-making process.
6. **Model Autonomy**: Lead by Example. Demonstrate autonomy in your actions and decision-making. Mentees often learn best by observing, so modeling autonomy sets a positive example for them to follow.
7. **Respect Different Approaches**: Diverse Perspectives: Understand that mentees may have different approaches and methods. Respect their unique ways of problem-

solving, allowing room for diverse perspectives and learning styles.
8. **Encourage Independent Thinking**: Mentorship is about empowering mentees to think for themselves. Encourage mentees to explore solutions independently and to trust their judgment.

Using skills discussed throughout this book such as clear communication, creating a supportive environment, and active listening the mentor/mentee can incorporate the above strategies into the mentorship plan at the appropriate time.

In conclusion, in Chapter 2 we learned that the mentor's/mentee's mindset is a powerful determinant of the mentorship experience. By cultivating a positive and supportive attitude, developing empathy and emotional intelligence, addressing bias, and balancing guidance with autonomy, mentors/mentees can create a transformative and enriching mentorship journey.

List of Chapter 2 Highpoints:
- Understanding the mentor's role is defined as shaping a mentee's personal and professional development with an emphasis on the importance of a positive and supportive approach.
- Emotional intelligence, particularly empathy, plays a crucial role in understanding and effectively responding to the mentee's needs and challenges.
- Unconscious biases can impact the mentorship relationship and need to be recognized and overcome to ensure fair and unbiased guidance.
- A balance between providing guidance and allowing autonomy must be established, allowing the mentee to make independent decisions and develop critical thinking skills.

Call to Action for the Mentor:

1. Regularly reflect on your mentoring approach and assess how your attitudes and actions affect your mentee. Identify areas for improvement.
2. Engage in activities that enhance your emotional intelligence, such as empathy training or active listening workshops.
3. Participate in a workshop or complete an online course on unconscious bias. Apply this knowledge to ensure your mentoring is fair and inclusive.
4. Incorporate open-ended, empowering questions in your discussions with mentees to encourage them to think independently and express their thoughts.
5. Establish a regular feedback loop with your mentee, encouraging honest and open communication to continually improve the mentorship dynamic.

Call to Action for the Mentee:

1. Clearly define your goals and share them with your mentor. Regularly review and adjust these goals as you progress.
2. Take an active role in the mentorship. Prepare for meetings with questions or topics for discussion.
3. Ask for feedback on your performance and strategies for improvement. Be open to receiving and acting on this feedback.
4. Before seeking your mentor's input on a challenge, attempt to produce solutions on your own. Discuss these solutions with your mentor to refine them.
5. Reflect on your personal growth throughout the mentorship. Identify key lessons learned and areas where you have developed.

Chapter Three: Finding the Right Mentor-Mentee Match

A. Identifying Mentorship Goals and Objectives

The foundation of a successful mentorship lies in planning. Included in planning should be the aligning of the goals and objectives of both the mentor and the mentee. Identifying these goals early in the mentorship process sets the stage for a purposeful and mutually beneficial relationship.

Defining Clear Objectives

Mentors and mentees will explore the importance of setting clear and specific objectives for the mentorship journey in the preliminary stages of mentorship and writing them down. There are numerous project management tools for this purpose such as Gantt Chart or Kanban board. Understanding each other's expectations and aspirations makes mentorship more targeted and impactful.

This section provides detailed information on how to establish clear objectives for mentorshipas follows:

1. **Understand the Mentee's Goals**: Begin by conducting a meeting to discuss and understand the mentee's professional and personal goals. A successful mentorship is tailored to the specific needs and aspirations of the mentee. This will take time and will require some prompting by the mentor through a series of questions. Explore the mentee's career ambitions, skill development needs, and areas for improvement. The goal is to identify the true goals of the mentee that will lead to their professional and personal development.

2. **Align with Organizational Objectives**: If not familiar already, the mentor will familiarize yourself with the organization's strategic priorities. With a good understanding of the mentee's goals, the mentor will ensure that the mentee's objectives align with the broader goals of the organization. Discuss how the mentee's goals can support or align with the organization's priorities. This integration fosters a mentorship that contributes to both individual and organizational success.

3. **Establish SMART Goals**: S.M.A.R.T. is an acronym that stands for Specific, Measurable, Achievable, Relevant, Time-Bound and are used to help guide goal setting and to increase the likelihood of achieving those goals. There are many resources to help you with SMART Goals so it will not be discussed in detail in this book. Clearly articulate goals using the SMART framework. This enhances accountability and provides a structured approach to achieving objectives. The mentor/mentee will collaborate to define specific and measurable goals ensuring that the goals are realistic, relevant to the mentee's role, and have a defined timeline.

4. **Prioritize Developmental Areas**: Conduct a skills assessment to identify key areas for the mentee's professional development. There are several skills assessments and more information on the type and conducting the assessment can be found on-line. This could include leadership skills, technical expertise, or interpersonal skills. It may include multiple goals and the mentor/mentee will have to prioritize the multiple goals considering predecessor goals. Some goals may have to precede others to ensure the success of all goals.

5. **Create a Development Plan**: A formal, documented roadmap is needed for success in mentorship. Develop a comprehensive plan outlining the steps and

milestones required to achieve the mentor's/mentee's objectives. Document these on the project tracking tool you are using. This plan serves as a roadmap for the mentorship journey. Do so through collaboration. Breakdown larger goals into smaller, achievable tasks as needed.

6. **Set Benchmarks for Progress**: Establish benchmarks to track mentorship progress including key performance indicators for each goal. Schedule regular check-ins to review progress, plan adjustments as agreed upon, and celebrate achievements to maintain motivation and momentum. Update the plan by maintaining a record of completed goals and achievements. This is motivational and will ensure that reward follows success.

7. **Include Soft Skills Development**: Identify those soft skills such as communication, emotional intelligence, leadership, finesse, poise, grace, style, smoothness, tactfulness, and diplomacy that will allow for holistic growth. Acknowledge the importance of soft skills development alongside technical or job-specific goals. Incorporate activities and feedback to enhance these skills. This contributes to the mentor's/mentee's overall professional growth.

8. **Encourage Networking and Exposure**: Building connections is a vital component to successful mentorship. The mentor will foster opportunities for the mentee to expand their professional network and gain exposure to various aspects of the organization or industry by recommending events, workshops, conferences, or industry forums for networking.

9. **Evaluate and Refine Objectives**: Seek to continuously improve by periodically assessing the effectiveness of the mentorship objectives by reviewing your project tracking tool. Especially early on, this will be a dynamic process. Solicit feedback from each other on the mentorship process. Be open to refining and

adjusting goals based on evolving needs and circumstances identified through your discussions.

Establishing clear objectives for mentorship at the onset involves a collaborative and structured approach. By aligning with the mentee's goals, integrating with organizational objectives, and incorporating feedback, the mentorship will be a dynamic and impactful experience for professional development for the mentor/mentee.

Goal Alignment for Success

In this section, we present some practical strategies to facilitate aligning mentorship goals, ensuring that the mentor's guidance is tailored to the mentee's professional and personal development needs. Clear goal alignment forms the basis for a focused and rewarding mentorship experience. We have already suggested using S.M.A.R.T. Goals so those will not be addressed here.

1. **Individual Development Plans (IDPs)**: These are a structured document outlining an individual's professional development goals and actions. This is developed at the onset of the mentorship and is dynamic, subject to change as the mentorship relationship matures over time. This requires collaboration and should not be done alone as a "homework" assignment. Be sure to include short-term and long-term goals, areas for development and action steps to achieve those goals.

2. **Strengths and Weaknesses Assessment**: May include tools such as StrengthsFinder, DISC assessment, Myers-Briggs Type Indicator (MBTI). These are particularly helpful if the mentor/mentee is uncertain about the goals and not able to clearly define the career path in which they are interested.

3. **Career Development Conversations**: These will be a routine part of mentorship. The conversations must be open and ongoing discussions about the mentee's career

aspirations, challenges, and goals. They may be slow at first until trust has been established and the mentor/mentee are in a comfortable environment. Regularly schedule dedicated sessions to discuss the mentee's evolving career objectives and how the mentor can support their growth.

4. **Feedback Mechanisms**: One helpful mechanism is called 360-Degree Feedback. This is a formal process that collects input from various sources, outside of the mentorship relationship including peers, supervisors, and subordinates. The feedback is given anonymously. It is something that can be used to create a benchmark for strengths and areas for improvement at the onset of the mentorship and then repeated later as a means of measuring success toward goals or it can be used later in the mentorship relationship again to measurement achievement toward goals.

5. **Personal Development Plans**: These are plans that focus on personal growth alongside professional development. The mentor works with the mentee to identify personal aspirations, such as work-life balance, stress management, or wellness goals, and integrate them into the mentorship plan.

6. **SWOT Analysis**: S.W.O.T. is an acronym that stands for Strengths, Weaknesses, Opportunities, and Threats. This type of analysis is more commonly known as a high-level planning model within organizations to identify where they are doing well and where they can improve from an internal and external perspective. In an analogous way S.W.O.T. analysis can be used to assess the mentee's professional profile, helping to shape goals and strategies for addressing challenges.

7. **Skill and Competency Frameworks:** Competency Models are used to help mentors understand the skills and competency of the mentee kas a way of defining areas for development in a particular field. There are

numerous plan types. One can be incorporated into the mentorship plan as an aid to the mentor.

8. **Action Learning Plans**: Sometimes called a M.A.P. or Mentorship Action Plan, these are structured plans that outline specific actions the mentee will take to achieve their goals. The mentor/mentee will collaborate on the action plan often breaking down larger goals into actionable steps, promoting continuous progress.

9. **Job Rotation or Shadowing Opportunities**: This is a straightforward way to broaden the mentee's perspective on the organization. This tool allows the mentee to experience distinct roles within the organization to broaden skills and perspectives. The mentor will help facilitate opportunities for job rotations or shadowing experiences to align with the mentee's career goals.

10. **Networking Events and Introductions**: Networking events within and external to the company are a wonderful way to encourage the mentee to participate in events or allow for introductions to relevant contacts in the industry or organization. The mentee must do the work in developing relationships outside of mentorship. The mentor can provide access to events, conferences, and introductions to key professionals.

11. **Regular Check-Ins and Progress Reviews**: As discussed throughout this book, mentorship includes regular planned and sometimes unplanned meetings to assess progress and discuss adjustments to goals. At a minimum, there should be a regular cadence for check-ins, allowing both mentor and mentee to review progress, address challenges, and refine goals as needed.

12. **Learning and Development Opportunities**: As areas for development are identified throughout mentorship, the mentor will encourage the mentee to participate in

workshops, courses, or seminars that align with the mentee's goals to enhance skills.

13. **Journaling and Reflection**: This is an activity that occurs outside of formal mentorship whereby the mentor will encourage regular reflection on experiences and insights require the mentee to maintain a journal of the reflections. The mentee will be directed to reflect on achievements, challenges, and personal growth, fostering self-awareness.

14. **Milestone Celebrations**: As discussed throughout this book there should be ongoing acknowledgment of significant achievements and milestones. The value of these celebrations should not be underestimated. Celebrate accomplishments along the mentorship journey to boost morale and reinforce the value of the mentorship.

By combining these tools and approaches, mentors and mentees can collaboratively design a mentorship plan that is tailored to the mentee's professional and personal goals. The key is to maintain open communication, regularly assess progress, and adapt the plan as the mentee's needs evolve.

B. Assessing Compatibility and Chemistry

The mentor-mentee relationship is a unique partnership that thrives on compatibility and chemistry. Assessing these factors is crucial for establishing a connection that fosters open communication and collaboration.

Compatibility Beyond Skills

While skills and expertise are essential, in this section we present some concepts to explore the broader aspects of compatibility, including values, communication styles, personality traits, emotional intelligence, work and learning styles, cultural competency, feedback and recognition preferences, and conflict resolution styles.

Mentors and mentees will learn to recognize the nuances that contribute to a harmonious and effective mentorship relationship, including the following.

1. **Values**: Values are fundamental beliefs or principles that guide an individual's behavior, decisions, and priorities. In mentorship, sharing values is important because it creates a foundation of mutual understanding and trust. Whereas misalignment in values may lead to conflicts or a lack of resonance in the mentorship relationship.

Mentors need to understand the values held by their mentee so they can tailor their guidance making sure it aligns with their core principles. Mentees must communicate their values openly, making sure the mento knows where they are coming from. This will allow the mentor to offer advice that respects and aligns with the value system of the mentee.

2. **Communication Styles**: Communication style refers to the way individuals express themselves, including verbal. and non-verbal cues, listening habits, and preferred modes of interaction. Working to establish compatible communication styles is important in mentorship to enhance effective and clear communication. Be open to new communication styles. Recognizing and adapting to unique styles improve the mentor-mentee dialogue.

Mentors need to be adaptable in their communication style to meet the mentee's preferences. Mentees should clearly express their communication preferences to ensure effective interaction. Both will need to spend time defining what those communication styles are and how best to achieve the needed best practices.

3. **Personality Traits**: Personality traits are enduring patterns of thoughts, feelings, and behaviors that influence how individuals perceive and interact with the world. They can be as unique as the individuals in the mentorship relationship. Complimentary personality traits can create a

balanced and dynamic mentorship relationship. Not every trait must be aligned to have an effective mentorship, but understanding each other's traits helps navigate potential conflicts and leverage strengths.

Mentors need to recognize and appreciate diverse personality traits in mentees and tailor their guidance accordingly. Mentees must endeavor to understand your mentor's personality, adapting to their style while maintaining authenticity.

4. **Emotional Intelligence**: Emotional intelligence involves recognizing, understanding, and managing one's own emotions and the emotions of others. In mentorship high emotional intelligence fosters empathy, trust, and effective communication. Each party to the mentorship should strive to high emotional intelligence. Bu doing so, mentors and mentees with strong emotional intelligence navigate challenges with resilience.

Mentors need to cultivate emotional intelligence to provide empathetic support. You must be prepared to be aware of, control, and express your emotions in a judicious and empathetic manner. Mentees must develop self-awareness and emotional regulation for constructive collaboration. Mentees may need to endeavor to control their emotions and not let your emotions control you.

5. **Work and Learning Styles**: Work and learning styles encompass preferences in how individuals approach tasks, problem-solving, and acquiring new skills. Mentors bring to mentorship proven styles for the experiences they have had. And too, they can share styles that should be avoided. Understanding work and learning styles enhances the effectiveness of mentorship strategies and helps to avoid unpleasant experiences. Sharing successful styles ensures that guidance and learning methods resonate with the mentee.

Mentors need to adapt mentoring approaches and to pull from their experience styles that match the mentee's work and learning preferences. Mentees must communicate their preferred work and learning styles for a tailored mentoring experience.

6. **Cultural Competence**: Cultural competence involves the ability to understand, respect, and effectively interact with individuals from diverse cultural backgrounds. This is a must-have in our growing culturally diverse workplaces and neighborhoods. Cultural competence promotes inclusivity and avoids misunderstandings in a diverse mentorship relationship. Some differences are obvious, others are more subtle. Recognizing cultural nuances enhances the mentor's ability to provide relevant guidance.

Mentors need to develop cultural competence to navigate diverse mentorship dynamics. This begins with being aware of and open to cultural diversity. Mentees must share insights about their cultural background to enrich the mentor's understanding and allow them to tailor their guidance to your strengths and skills.

7. **Feedback and Recognition Preferences**: Feedback and recognition preferences are the preferences for how individuals give and receive feedback, as well as their preferred methods of recognition. This will vary with personality type. Some people are already tough on themselves so how feedback is delivered needs to take this into account. Remember, **feedback is not always positive, but it should always be delivered positively**. And too, some people are extremely comfortable with recognition, while others do not like the spotlight. Understanding feed-back preferences enhances the mentor's ability to provide constructive guidance. Recognizing and acknowledging achievements in alignment with preferences boost motivation.

Mentors need to adapt their feedback styles to resonate with the mentee and vice versa. Mentors must come to the realization that the same recognition cannot be used in all instances. Mentors will have to tailor recognition approaches to align with the mentees' preferences. Mentees must make no assumptions that their mentor will know their preferences. Communicate your preferences for feedback and recognition.

8. **Conflict Resolution Styles**: Conflict resolution styles are the approaches individuals take to resolve conflicts or disagreements. These will arise in mentorship where open communication is encouraged. Compatible conflict resolution styles contribute to a healthy and constructive mentorship relationship. Understanding each other's approaches prevents misunderstandings during challenging times. Exercise patience.

Mentors will need to recognize and adapt to the mentee's conflict resolution style. Mentees: Be aware of your own style and communicate it to facilitate effective conflict resolution. There is a fabulous resource if you are being challenged in the area called, Crucial Conversations for Mastering Dialogue[12]. It is available as on-demand learning or as a book. Would strongly encourage all those reading this book to request that their companies require completion of this course by all employees.

In summary, compatibility in mentorship extends beyond professional goals to encompass values, communication styles, personality traits, emotional intelligence, work and learning styles, cultural competency, feedback and recognition preferences, and conflict resolution styles. A nuanced understanding of these aspects allows mentors and mentees to build a relationship rooted in mutual respect, effective communication, and shared understanding. Regular dialogue and openness to learning from one another contribute to the richness of the mentorship experience. Make it a win/win.

Building Chemistry for Engagement

Building a rapport and fostering chemistry between mentors and mentees enhances engagement and trust. The following practical tips are provided as a guide on how to establish a comfortable and collaborative dynamic that encourages open dialogue and shared learning experiences. If you are familiar with other sections of this book you will start to see a commonality in the tips provided.

Building rapport in mentorship is essential for establishing a comfortable, inclusive, and collaborative dynamic between mentors and mentees. A strong rapport encourages open dialogue and shared learning experiences.

This subpart is separated by tips for the mentor, tips for the mentee, and joint actions to foster a positive mentorship relationship:

For Mentors

1. **Create a Welcoming Environment**: Initiate conversations in a warm and friendly manner. Make mentees feel comfortable from the start. Successful mentorship requires a time commitment from you. Enjoy this opportunity to guide and help someone. Begin meetings with a casual check-in, inquire about the mentee's well-being, and show genuine interest in their experiences.

2. **Active Listening**: Demonstrate active listening by maintaining eye contact, nodding, and providing verbal affirmations. Be sincere. Repeat key points the mentee shares to show understanding and validate their perspectives.

3. **Share Personal Experiences**: Be transparent about your own experiences, challenges, and learning moments. Do not be afraid to share. Share relevant anecdotes to illustrate points, making the mentorship relationship more relatable.

4. **Establish Clear Communication Norms**: Discuss communication preferences, frequency of meetings, and preferred methods of contact. Get this down early in the mentorship. It may change as the mentorship matures. That is okay but agree on the expectations early on to ensure a mutual understanding of how communication will flow.

5. **Encourage Questions and Curiosity**: Create an environment where mentees feel comfortable asking questions and expressing curiosity. This will help to spark ideas. Actively encourage questions and provide thoughtful responses that promote learning. If you do not know or cannot remember you can always follow up at the next meeting or before.

6. **Acknowledge and Celebrate Achievements**: Recognize and celebrate both small and significant achievements of the mentee taking into consideration recognition preferences. If you do not know what these are, talk about it with the mentee. Take time to acknowledge milestones, and express genuine enthusiasm for their progress.

7. **Respect and Value Diversity**: Embrace and appreciate the diversity of perspectives, experiences, and backgrounds. Foster inclusivity by recognizing and valuing the unique contributions each mentee brings to the mentorship relationship. There is always something to be learned. Just be open to it.

8. **Provide Constructive Feedback**: Offer feedback in a constructive and supportive manner, focusing on growth opportunities. Be sure to consider the feedback preferences of the mentee. If you do not know what these are, talk about it with the mentee. Frame feedback as a tool for development and improvement, emphasizing specific areas for enhancement. Assess the acceptance of the feedback provided.

For Mentees:

1. **Express Your Goals and Expectations**: Clearly communicate your professional and personal goals to your mentor. Remember, your mentor is there to guide and support. If you do not share openly, they will not know what you are seeking and may not guide you as you want resulting in conflict. One of their skills is not mind reading. Share your expectations for the mentorship relationship, ensuring alignment with your aspirations.

2. **Initiate Communication**: Take the initiative to reach out to your mentor and schedule regular check-ins. For some this may be a challenge. The mentor is there for you, and they have your best interest in mind. Do not think that your formal meetings are your only opportunity to communicate with your mentor. Make sure you have agreed to an open-door policy. Seek advice, always. By doing so, you will demonstrate your commitment to the mentorship by actively initiating discussions and planning.

3. **Be Open to Feedback**: Approach feedback with an open mindset, viewing it as an opportunity for growth. If you do not like how it is being delivered share your feedback preferences with your mentor. Do not just listen and "take it on the chin." **Feedback is not always positive, but it should always be delivered in a positive way**. Act on constructive feedback provided by your mentor and use it as a catalyst for improvement.

4. **Show Gratitude**: Express gratitude for your mentor's time, guidance, and support. They are sharing their guidance and experience with you, sometime gained through trial and error, so that you do not have that same experience. Acknowledge the value of your mentor's contributions and demonstrate appreciation for their mentorship.

5. **Be Proactive in Learning**: Take the initiative to seek additional resources, attend relevant events, and continuously learn. You have communicated your willingness to be mentored and will dedicate a lot of time to your success. If you want to be successful in your career path, get to work. Demonstrate an initiative-taking attitude toward your own professional development.

6. **Share Challenges and Seek Advice**: Openly discuss challenges you are facing and seek your mentor's advice. Regardless of where you are in your mentorship, challenges are NOT failures. Use mentorship as a safe space to share concerns, allowing your mentor to provide guidance and perspective. They have the same challenges.

7. **Participate Actively in Discussions**: Engage actively in discussions, ask thoughtful questions, and contribute to conversations. Do not waste your time and that of the mentor. If you are not into the conversation, let them know. Share with them why you are not into the mentorship. Contribute your insights and experiences, fostering a collaborative and dynamic mentorship relationship.

8. **Reflect on Mentoring Insights**: Reflect on the insights gained from mentoring sessions and incorporate them into your professional journey. If you are having difficulty doing so, consider that you may not have communicated well what you are looking for. Backup and represent your expectations to clarify what you are seeking. Use mentorship as an opportunity for self-reflection and personal development.

Joint Actions:
1. **Establish Mutual Goals**: Collaboratively set goals that align with both the mentor's and mentee's objectives. Consider the idea presented earlier that you

are in a mentee/mentee relationship whereby both learn and develop. Work together to define clear and measurable outcomes that contribute to your collective growth.

2. **Regularly Assess and Adjust**: Periodically assess the effectiveness of the mentorship relationship. It is dynamic and should change as does any relationship. Have open discussions about what is working well and areas that may need adjustment or improvement. Set aside periodically meetings for this purpose.

3. **Create a Feedback Loop**: Establish a feedback loop where both mentor and mentee can share thoughts on the mentorship in a comfortable and safe environment. Encourage honest and constructive feedback, ensuring continuous improvement in the relationship.

4. **Celebrate Diversity and Inclusion**: Embrace and celebrate diversity in all its forms. There is so much to learn from respecting differences. Keep it positive and constructive. Create an inclusive environment that values diverse perspectives and fosters a sense of belonging for all participants.

5. **Encourage Peer Learning**: Facilitate opportunities for learning by those outside of the mentorship. Do not limit the advances you will make to only the mentorship. Lead the way in your organization to bold improvements. Encourage each other to share insights and experiences, promoting a community of shared learning.

6. **Promote a Growth Mindset**: Foster a growth mindset, emphasizing the belief that abilities and intelligence can be developed and shared. Encourage each other to view challenges as opportunities for learning and growth.

By incorporating these practical tips, mentors and mentees can cultivate a strong rapport that supports a positive and mutually beneficial mentorship relationship. The emphasis on communication, mutual respect, and shared learning experiences contributes to a collaborative dynamic that fosters professional and personal development.

C. Balancing Diversity in Mentorship

Diversity in mentorship is not just about checking boxes; it is about leveraging a variety of perspectives and experiences to enrich the mentorship journey. Balancing diversity ensures a well-rounded and inclusive approach to mentorship.

Embracing Diversity of Thought

Mentors and mentees will explore the benefits of embracing diversity of thought, experiences, and backgrounds in mentorship. This section will provide insights into how a diverse mentorship pairing can lead to innovative solutions and a broader understanding of the professional landscape.

Embracing diversity of thought, experiences, and backgrounds in mentorship can lead to a multitude of benefits, including the generation of innovative solutions and a broader understanding of the professional landscape.

Here are insights into how a diverse mentorship pairing can contribute to these positive outcomes:

1. **Rich Pool of Perspectives**: Diverse mentorship pairs bring together individuals with different life experiences, cultural backgrounds, and professional journeys. This diversity enriches discussions by providing a broader range of perspectives, enabling the exploration of creative and varied solutions to challenges. Both parties must be open to the richness that comes from these discussions.

2. **Innovative Problem-Solving**: Diverse mentorship fosters a culture of innovative problem-solving. The "same-old/same-old" is not the universal fix. The

melding of varied viewpoints encourages mentors and mentees to approach challenges from different angles, leading to innovative solutions that may not have been considered in a more homogeneous pairing. Have the courage to approach problem solving with an open mind. The solution may come from the less experienced person.

3. **Cultural Competence Development**: Diverse mentorship exposes individuals to diverse cultural norms, values, and communication styles. Mentees gain valuable insights into navigating diverse professional environments, promoting cultural competence that is essential in today's globalized workplace. Mentors gain valuable insight by sharing what has worked successfully and guiding the mentee to avoid the pitfalls they experienced.

4. **Enhanced Creativity and Innovation**: Diversity in mentorship cultivates a dynamic environment where creativity can flourish. Exposure to a variety of thought processes sparks creativity, fostering an atmosphere conducive to innovation and out-of-the-box thinking. Even in regulated industries, creativity should not be stifled but allowed to flourish under the guidance of the mentor.

5. **Cross-Pollination of Skills**: Diverse mentorship allows for the exchange of skills and knowledge from different fields. Mentors and mentees can leverage cross-disciplinary insights, applying skills from one domain to innovate and solve challenges in another.

6. **Increased Cultural Awareness**: Diverse mentorship pairs contribute to increased cultural awareness. Mentees not only benefit from the mentor's guidance but also gain exposure to diverse ways of working and thinking, fostering a more inclusive and globally aware mindset.

7. **Breaking Stereotypes**: Diverse mentorship challenges and breaks down stereotypes. Mentors and mentees, by working together across diverse backgrounds, contribute to dismantling preconceived notions, fostering a culture of inclusivity, and understanding.

8. **Improved Decision-Making**: Diverse mentorship promotes more informed decision-making. By considering a variety of perspectives, mentors and mentees can make decisions that are well-rounded, reflective of diverse viewpoints, and more likely to lead to successful outcomes.

9. **Diversity of Networks**: Diverse mentorship expands professional networks. Mentees gain access to the mentor's diverse network, providing opportunities to connect with individuals from various industries, backgrounds, and career levels.

10. **Global Perspective**: Diverse mentorship contributes to a global perspective. Exposure to diverse experiences and backgrounds prepares mentees for a globalized professional landscape, where understanding and navigating various perspectives is increasingly important.

11. **Fostering Inclusive Leadership**: Diverse mentorship models inclusive leadership behaviors. Mentors, through their diverse experiences, serve as role models for inclusive leadership, emphasizing the value of diversity and promoting an inclusive and supportive professional environment.

12. **Enhanced Problem Definition**: Diverse perspectives contribute to a more nuanced problem definition. A diverse mentorship pairing ensures a comprehensive understanding of challenges, allowing for a more accurate and thorough definition of problems before attempting to solve them.

13. **Resilience and Adaptability**: Exposure to diverse experiences builds resilience and adaptability. Mentees develop resilience by navigating diverse challenges, learning to adapt to different working styles, and gaining skills that are transferable across varied contexts.

14. **Encouraging Inclusivity in Teams**: Diverse mentorship fosters inclusivity within teams. Mentees, having experienced the benefits of diversity in their mentorship, are more likely to champion inclusivity within their own teams, creating a positive ripple effect.

15. **Preparation for Future Leadership Roles**: Diverse mentorship prepares individuals for future leadership roles. Exposure to diverse perspectives equips mentees with the skills and insights needed to lead in an increasingly diverse and complex professional landscape.

In conclusion, diverse mentorship pairings not only contribute to innovative solutions and a broader understanding of the professional landscape but also play a pivotal role in shaping inclusive leaders and fostering a culture of creativity, adaptability, and resilience in the workplace. The benefits extend beyond the mentorship relationship, positively impacting organizational culture and contributing to a more equitable and forward-thinking professional community.

Addressing Unconscious Bias

Recognizing and addressing unconscious bias is essential for creating a mentorship environment that is equitable and inclusive. Strategies for overcoming biases and promoting diversity in mentorship will be discussed, allowing mentors and mentees to cultivate a richer and more expansive mentorship experience.

Unconscious bias refers to the automatic, unintentional attitudes or stereotypes that affect our understanding, actions, and decisions unconsciously. These biases can be based on several factors, such as gender, race, age, or other characteristics. In mentorship, unconscious bias can impact the mentor-mentee relationship, potentially hindering diversity, equity, and inclusion. To cultivate a richer and more expansive mentorship experience, it is essential to recognize and address unconscious bias.

Here are insights into different forms of unconscious bias and strategies for overcoming them in mentorship:

Forms of Unconscious Bias (refer to Chapter 2, Section C for more on bias):

1. **Affinity Bias**: Preference is given to individuals with the same or similar backgrounds, experience, or characteristics. In mentorship, this may lead to mentors/mentees favoring their counterparts who are like them. This will lead to limiting diversity in the mentorship relationship and may result in perpetuation of unfavorable biases.

2. **Confirmation Bias**: Giving more weight to information that confirms existing beliefs. This bias refers to the tendency of individuals to favor, interpret, and remember information in a way that confirms their preexisting beliefs or hypotheses. In mentorship, this may lead to mentors/mentees to reinforce preconceived notions about certain groups, limiting the mentor's/mentee's potential to grow from the mentorship.

3. **Halo Effect**: Occurs when positive impressions in one area leads to an overall positive judgment of a person. Mentors/mentees may overlook areas of improvement or development in a mentor/mentee due to an overall positive impression.

4. **Similarity Bias**: Preferring individuals who are like oneself in terms of background, interest, or values. This often makes us feel "comfortable" but may result in

mentors/mentees selecting the other who resemble them, perpetuating a lack of diversity and limiting the full experience that successful mentorship offers.

5. **Attribution Bias**: This occurs when the mentor/mentee attributes positive actions to their own character and negative actions to external factors. This will lead to unfair judgments about the mentor's/mentee's ability or performance. This will manifest itself particularly during feedback where negativity reigns supreme.

Strategies for Overcoming Unconscious Bias in Mentorship:

1. **Increase Awareness**: If your company does not offer awareness education and training, one strategy is for the mentor/mentee to seek the training themselves by engaging in external workshops, discussion, and readings that highlight the impact of bias in mentorship and promote self-awareness. Equip yourselves with tools to identify and challenge your own biases, fostering a more inclusive and equitable mentorship experience.

2. **Implement Blind Matching**: In companies with formal mentorship programs a technique called blind matching can be used that pairs mentors and mentees without disclosing certain demographic information. Identifiers such as gender or ethnicity are removed during the initial match process. Companies without a formal program whereby the mentor/mentee pairing is organic, mentor/mentee should encourage awareness of bias as described above.

3. **Structured Mentorship Programs**: Companies with formal mentoring programs should provide clearly outlined objectives, expectations, and evaluation criteria to ensure a fair and standardized approach to mentorship. Companies without a formal mentorship

program should adopt a more formalized approach to ensure mentorship success.

4. **Diverse Mentorship Panels**: Create diverse mentorship panels or committees responsible for mentorship pairings making sure the decision-making process involves individuals with diverse perspectives to mitigate individual biases.

5. **Promote Open Communication**: Whether the company you are in has a formal mentorship program or not, a cornerstone to successful mentorship is open communication. This will allow mentor and mentee to address potential biases. Encourage each other to express your goals, aspirations, and concerns. By doing so you will create an environment for honest discussions about bias.

6. **Mentorship Diversity Goals**: When developing your mentorship plans set specific goals for mentorship diversity. Establish metrics and include them in your plan. For example, plan to attend one or more bias awareness training workshops within six months of initiating the mentorship program.

7. **Encourage Cross-Cultural Experiences**: Mentorship is a terrific opportunity to learn something new about a different culture. Encourage each other to engage in cross-cultural experiences. Fairs, art shows, music, cuisine, and dance are some examples. Exposure to diverse cultures and perspectives will broaden understanding and reduce unconscious biases.

8. **Feedback and Evaluation**: Another pillar to successful mentorship is feedback and evaluation. Include in your mentorship plan regular opportunities for feedback and evaluations. This is intended for both parties to the mentorship. The mentor and mentee are encouraged to provide feedback on the mentorship

relationship, helping to identify and address perceived biases as they arise.

9. **Establish Inclusive Mentorship Resources**: Related to bias awareness, include in your mentorship reading materials, case studies, or resources that emphasize the benefits of diverse mentorship relationships.

10. **Create Safe Spaces for Dialogue**: Another cornerstone to successful mentorship is creating a safe space for dialogue. Both mentor and mentee must feel that the relationship is one where trust and respect prevail. Only then can true open discussion exist allowing both parties to discuss biases openly. Both must feel comfortable acknowledging and addresses biases without fear of judgment.

11. **Accountability Measures**: You have established the type of mentorship that will take place, you have put together a plan, you have undergone some bias awareness training, established goals including diversity goals, created an understanding that the mentorship is safe to encourage open discussion, and now you need to implement accountability measures. This should not be burdensome but will hold each party accountable for adhering to inclusive practices and addressing biases, creating a culture of responsibility.

By implementing these strategies, mentors and mentees can work collaboratively to identify and overcome unconscious bias in their mentorship relationships. This not only enriches the mentorship experience but also contributes to a more inclusive, equitable, and diverse professional landscape.

D. The Role of Trust in the Mentor-Mentee Dynamic

Trust forms the bedrock of a successful mentor-mentee relationship. Understanding the dynamics of trust and how to cultivate it is pivotal for creating a safe and supportive mentorship environment.

Building Trust Through Transparency

Transparency in communication and actions is key to building trust and is crucial for success. Transparency, openness, and honesty contribute to a trusting relationship, allowing mentees to feel secure in seeking guidance and feedback. The mentor will be rewarded by improving the mentee's experience and business performance.

But where does this begin or how can the mentor begin to build trust through transparency? In this section, we will present ways that mentors/mentees can build trust through transparency. We will focus on one of the ways presented in particular - an "open door policy." As you will learn this requires commitment and should include all employees, not just the mentee.

This can be further enhanced by having a policy of weekly office hours where all employees are welcome, not just the mentee, to bring their thoughts, ideas, and yes concerns.

Here are ways that mentors and mentees can build trust through transparency:

For Mentors:
1. **Share Personal Experiences**: Early in the mentorship relationship sharing firsthand experiences may be intimidating, but do not be afraid to open up. Mentors, open up about your own career journey, challenges faces, and lessons learned from your successes/failures. Sharing firsthand experiences makes the mentor/mentee relatable and demonstrates vulnerability, fostering a sense of trust.

2. **Clarify Expectations**: Clarify and establish your expectations for the mentorship relationship. By setting expectations from the beginning, mentees understand

what to expect, promoting a transparent and accountable partnership.

3. **Be Open About Limitations**: Everyone has limitations. Be transparent with the mentee by acknowledging areas where you may not have expertise or experience. You may find areas where you both can build upon as part of the mentorship. Demonstrate humility and honesty about your limitations as a way of helping to build trust. This will show that you are genuine and fallible.

4. **Provide Constructive Feedback**: Provide feedback in a constructive and positive manner. No one appreciates being belittled or put down. Honest feedback, delivered with empathy, builds the other person, and reinforces a mentorship relationship built on trust. **Feedback is not always positive, but it should always be delivered in a positive way.**

5. **Share Decision-Making Processes**: It is easy to bark directions or be demanding of the mentee, but that does not lead to trust or an enduring mentorship. Rather, be transparent when discussing decisions by sharing your thought processes and considerations. This will provide insight into your decision-making style, foster transparency and clarify any uncertainty the mentee may have but is unwilling to share.

6. **Admit Mistakes and Learnings**: No one is perfect and should never be perceived as such. Own any mistakes past and present. Do so by discussing mistakes made before or during mentorship. You will see that there are a lot of similarities in your careers. Admit mistakes and share the lessons learned. This will demonstrate humility and authenticity, contributing to trust.

7. **Open Door Policy**: This is more than just setting hours to meet and leaving your door open during the day.

This is helpful, but mentees need to know they can approach you with questions, challenges, concerns, or feedback anytime. Tell them and encourage them to do so. Creating a true open-door policy promotes transparency and shows that you value them as a person as well as open communication.

For Mentees:

1. **Communicate Goals and Aspirations**: Come prepared to each meeting with the mentor to clearly articulate your professional and personal goals, challenges, and concerns. This may require some homework, sitting down and writing in a journal or some other way of documenting your needs and concerns. Develop the habit of doing so before each mentorship meeting. Being prepared will allow you to express your aspirations more openly. When clearly articulated, you will help your mentor to understand how to tailor their guidance to your specific needs.

2. **Share Challenges and Concerns**: Mentees, open up about your weaknesses, concerns, goals, and challenges. Your mentor is someone who has climbed over the mountain you are facing. Discuss challenges and concerns with clarity and provide relevant examples in your career to allow the mentor to provide targeted support and guidance.

3. **Express Learning Needs**: You may be new to the department or the organization. Communicate areas where you feel you need further development or knowledge. Your mentor will actively listen to identify gaps that may prevent your success. By being transparent on what you believe are your learning needs will help your mentor tailor their guidance to address the specific gaps that you agree upon.

4. **Seek Feedback Actively**: Do not wait for it. Be sure that your mentorship plan includes periodic feedback on your performance in your job and your role in the

mentorship process and to identify areas for improvement. By demonstrating a willingness to receive feedback you will foster a transparent and growth-oriented mentorship relationship.

5. **Be Open to Mentor's Guidance**: Early in the mentorship relationship you may find that you are hesitant or uncertain about guidance from your mentor. You may think that they do not know well enough your situation. Be receptive to your mentor's advice and guidance. You will see over time they have your best interest at heart. Openness to mentorship signals that you value the mentor's expertise, contributing to a trusting relationship.

6. **Discuss Career Choices and Concerns**: For some, this may be a moving target at first or there is a fair amount of uncertainty. That is okay. For others, you may be very certain of where you want to go and only need direction and guidance to get there. In either case, engage in open conversations about your career choices, concerns, and dilemmas. Transparency about career decisions helps mentors provide guidance that aligns with your values and aspirations.

7. **Update on Progress**: Tell them how you see your progress. If you have a disappointment or triumph between meetings, let them know about it. Regularly update your mentor on your progress, achievements, and challenges. Keeping your mentor informed fosters a transparent relationship and allows for relevant, timely guidance and celebration.

Joint Actions:
1. **Regular Check-Ins**: Regular check-ins should be built into the mentorship plan. Mentor/mentee are responsible to ensure that regular check-ins are planned and documented to allow for open communication about progress, challenges, and goals. Consistent communication promotes transparency and helps

mentors/mentees to stay informed about each other's experiences.

2. **Honest Conversations**: The mentorship relationship is no place for not sharing. Encourage and engage each other in honest, open conversations. Open, honest dialogue builds trust by fostering an environment where mentor/mentee feel comfortable sharing thoughts, concerns, and insights even at times when sharing is uncomfortable.

3. **Establish Confidentiality Guidelines**: This may be a tough one even in a world where nothing is confidential. Begin by clearly communicating expectations regarding confidentiality. Remind each other periodically what is confidential and discuss how the information can be used. Do not assume. Establishing and keeping confidentiality guidelines ensures that sensitive information can be shared safely, fostering trust in the mentorship relationship.

4. **Jointly Set Boundaries**: Get the mentorship off on the right start. Establish this early on the mentorship so there are no misunderstandings that result in hard feelings. Collaboratively set boundaries regarding communication frequency and methods as well as personal time. Establishing clear boundaries is healthy ensuring that both parties are comfortable with the level of interaction, contributing to a transparent relationship.

5. **Celebrate Successes Together**: Celebrating success and reaching milestones is an essential component to mentorship and building trust. Celebrate successes together. This will strengthen the mentorship bond and reinforce trust in a positive and collaborative environment.

In summary, transparency builds trust by creating an environment where mentors and mentees can openly communicate, share experiences, and work collaboratively toward common goals. Openness and honesty contribute to the authenticity of the mentorship relationship, fostering mutual respect and a sense of security that is essential for long-term success.

Nurturing Trust Over Time

The mentorship relationship must evolve. Be patient. Rome was not built in a day. One attribute of the mentorship relationship is trust. Trust is not instantaneous; it evolves. We present below some strategies that the mentor/mentee can explore for nurturing trust throughout the mentorship journey, including consistent communication, reliability, and the demonstration of genuine care and support.

Here are strategies for fostering trust in mentorship over time. You will note that each strategy contains elements presented above, defined in more detail. These are not one and done. They need to be practiced and developed over time.

1. **Consistent communication**: Regular communication is key to building trust in a mentor-mentee relationship. It is important to establish a communication schedule that works for both parties and stick to it. This can be done through regular check-ins, emails, or phone calls. It is also important to be responsive and timely in your communication.

2. **Reliability**: Being reliable is another key factor in building trust. This means showing up to meetings prior to the start time, following through on commitments, doing your homework and meeting preparation, and being accountable for your actions. If you say you will do something, make sure you do it. If you cannot fulfill a commitment, communicate this to your mentee as soon as possible.

3. **Demonstration of genuine care and support**: Showing genuine care and support for the other in mentorship can help build trust. This can be done by actively listening to your mentee, providing

constructive feedback, and offering guidance and advice when needed. Ask questions to promote thought, participation, and ideas. It is also important to be empathetic and understanding of your mentee's needs and concerns.

These strategies can help build a solid foundation of trust in a mentor-mentee relationship. However, it is important to remember that trust takes time to develop and requires ongoing effort to maintain.

In summary, trust in mentorship is built over time through consistent communication, reliability, and a genuine demonstration of care and support. Mentors and mentees who prioritize these strategies contribute to the development of a trusting relationship that is resilient, adaptable, and conducive to long-term professional and personal growth.

In conclusion, in Chapter 3 we learned that finding the right mentor-mentee match is a nuanced process that involves aligning goals, assessing compatibility, embracing diversity, and cultivating trust. Using the strategies presented in this chapter mentor/mentee can navigate these elements thoughtfully and can lay the groundwork for a rewarding and transformative mentorship relationship.

List of Chapter 3 Highpoints:
- Mentors and mentees MUST clearly define their goals and objectives for the mentorship to ensure alignment and focused direction.
- The compatibility and chemistry between a mentor and a mentee are crucial for a successful relationship, affecting communication, trust, and the overall effectiveness of the mentorship.
- There are benefits of diversity in mentorship, including varied perspectives, experiences, and the opportunity for challenging preconceived notions and biases.

- The role of trust in the mentor-mentee dynamic is a corner stone that needs to be built in the beginning of the mentorship relationship and maintained throughout the journey.

Call to Action for the Mentor:
1. Clearly articulate what you can offer as a mentor, including your areas of expertise, experience, and the mentoring style you prefer.
2. When considering a mentee, assess compatibility in terms of goals, values, and communication styles to ensure a productive relationship.
3. Participate in diversity training to understand how different perspectives can enrich the mentorship experience.
4. Be consistent in your interactions and follow through on commitments to build and maintain trust with your mentee.
5. Establish open lines of communication, encouraging your mentees to share their thoughts and feedback about the mentorship.

Call to Action for the Mentee:
1. Clearly define and communicate your goals for seeking a mentor. Understand what you want to achieve through mentorship.
2. Consider choosing a mentor who may offer a unique perspective than your own, to broaden your understanding and challenge your viewpoints.
3. When selecting a mentor, consider how their experience, communication style, and mentoring approach align with your learning style and goals.
4. Be open, honest, and consistent in your interactions with your mentor to help establish a foundation of trust.
5. Regularly give feedback to your mentor about what is working well and what might be improved in the mentorship relationship.

Chapter Four: Establishing Clear Goals and Expectations

In Mentorship Mastery, the key to a successful mentorship lies in the clarity and alignment of goals and expectations. This chapter is dedicated to the meticulous process of defining, setting, and managing these elements for a purposeful and effective mentorship journey.

A. Defining Short-Term and Long-Term Goals

Short-Term Goals: A Path to Quick Wins

In this section we will explore the significance of short-term goals in providing quick wins and building momentum. Setting achievable, bite-sized goals allows for an immediate sense of accomplishment, fostering motivation and enthusiasm. The significance of short-term goals in mentorship lies in their ability to demonstrate progress, instill a sense of purpose, and build a positive trajectory for the mentor-mentee relationship.

One crucial aspect of short-term goals is their ability to establish an early connection between mentor and mentee. By focusing on achievable goals, mentors can highlight their commitment to the mentee's development and provide a glimpse into the tangible benefits of mentorship. For mentees, these initial wins serve as confidence boosters, validating their decision to seek guidance and reaffirming the mentorship's value.

Examples of Short-Term Goals in Mentorship:

1. **Skills Enhancement**: Start with baby steps. Identify and focus on one specific skill for improvement within the next month. It does not have to reach finality, but this short-term goal should allow the mentee to see immediate progress in a targeted area and demonstrate

to the mentor their commitment to improvement and mentorship. Its public speaking, time management, learning a new system or technical skill relevant to their field.

2. **Networking Opportunities**: Networking is an essential aspect of mentorship. With all the social platforms today, it is easy to connect with a specified number of professionals in the industry within two (2) weeks. The mentor can introduce the mentee to new contacts and the mentee can search on their own. Remember the proper etiquette when connecting with professional contracts. Actively expanding the mentee's professional network provides a quick win in terms of new connections, potential mentors, and opportunities for collaboration.

3. **Goal Setting and Planning**: Again, use baby steps. Decide on a reasonable short-term goal and action plan. Start with three (3) months. Working together setting a short-term goal and action plan establishes a structure approach to mentorship and reinforces the importance of goal setting for your mutual success.

4. **Feedback Implementation**: Within your short-term goal and action plan allow time for feedback to a specific project or task immediately following the due date. Actively applying feedback following the completion of the project or task provides immediate results, highlighting the impact of mentorship on skill refinement and project outcomes.

5. **Knowledge Acquisition**: The objective here is to complete a short online course or attend a relevant workshop within the next month. Acquiring new knowledge and skills in a brief period demonstrates the mentor's commitment to support the mentee and the mentee's commitment to continuous learning and professional development.

6. **Career Exploration**: This exercise allows the mentees to go into other departments and distinct roles within the organization. This helps to broaden perspective and explore various facets of the professional landscape allowing for quick insights into diverse career paths and helps to shape long-term career goals. Include the results of this exercise in a mentorship meeting.

7. **Time Management Strategies**: Discuss the time management strategies each of you use. There are many available today. Agree on one or more that can be implemented in the next two (2) weeks that are not being used. Examples include, start your day with a plan, prioritize the most important tasks, divide larger projects into smaller ones, take breaks, and limit distractions. Enhancing time management skills provides an immediate impact on productivity and work-life balance, contributing to the overall effectiveness of the mentee.

8. **Networking Event Attendance**: Get out of the office and spread your wings. Agree on a relevant industry networking event and attend it within the next month. The mentor is a valuable resource for such events and may know of one that they found rewarding. By actively participating in industry events the mentee will quickly expand their network, fostering connections that can lead to potential opportunities.

9. **Professional Branding**: A professional brand statement is needed to be successful and recognized on social platforms. It is a brief statement that summarizes who you are as a professional, what you do, and what differentiates you from others in your field. Both the mentor and mentee need a professional brand statement and can work on this together. Create one and optimize your social media platforms within the next three (3) weeks. This will ensure that both of you are well-positioned for networking and career advancement.

10. **Project Collaboration**: Great opportunity to collaborate on a small-scale project together, implementing share insights and strategies. Examples may include developing a personal brand statement (sound familiar?), volunteering, or a small-scale research project. Working together on a project provides firsthand experience, allowing both mentor and mentee to witness the immediate impact of their collaboration.

In conclusion, short-term goals in mentorship are instrumental in providing quick wins, building momentum, and establishing a positive foundation for the mentor-mentee relationship. These objectives serve as steppingstones, fostering a sense of achievement and motivation that propels both mentors and mentees toward more significant, long-term goals.

Long-Term Goals: The North Star

In this section, we explore the long-term goals and how they serve as the guiding force for the mentorship journey. We will delve into the process of collaboratively defining ambitious yet attainable long-term goals that align with the mentee's overarching career and personal development aspirations. Long-term goals shape the broader narrative of mentorship, providing a framework for comprehensive transformation and achievement. The significance of long-term goals lies in their ability to create a sense of purpose, inspire commitment, and foster a deepened mentor-mentee connection over the course of the mentorship journey.

Examples of Long-Term Goals in Mentorship:

1. **Career Advancement to Leadership Role:** The mentee aims to transition from a team member to a leadership position within five years with the purpose to cultivate leadership skills and experience necessary for career progression.

2. **Mastering a New Professional Skill or Area of Expertise:** Over the next three years the mentee

intends to become proficient in a new, valuable skill set (e.g., digital marketing) relevant to their field to expand and diversify professional capabilities.

3. **Personal Development and Emotional Intelligence Growth:** The mentee will enhance emotional intelligence (EI) to improve interpersonal relationships and team dynamics over four years to develop a deeper understanding of self and others.

4. **Building a Professional Network and Personal Brand:** To create valuable connections and establish credibility and visibility in the industry the mentee aims to expand their professional network and establish a strong personal brand within the industry over the next five years.

These examples of long-term goals in mentorship embody a framework for comprehensive transformation and achievement, and they are designed to inspire purpose, and commitment, and foster a deepened connection between the mentor and mentee.

Process of Collaboratively Defining Long-Term Goals:

1. **Mentee Self-Reflection**: Initiation Point. Allow time for this. The process begins with the mentee engaging in thorough self-reflection. This involves assessing current skills, strengths, weaknesses, and identifying long-term career and personal development aspirations. This is your time to set down what you want to achieve in your career. Take this seriously and no idea is a bad idea.

2. **Goal Identification**: This is when collaboration begins. The mentor and mentee engage in open and reflective discussions to identify specific long-term goals. These goals should align with the mentee's overarching career aspirations and personal

development vision. A bonus to this process is that you will get to know one another as more than just co-workers.

3. **S.W.O.T. Analysis**: Let us get strategic! Conduct a collaborative SWOT (Strengths, Weaknesses, Opportunities, Threats) analysis to understand the current landscape. This analysis informs the selection of goals that leverage strengths, address weaknesses, capitalize on opportunities, and mitigate potential threats.

4. **S.M.A.R.T. Criteria**: Agree upon and establish long-term objectives using the SMART criteria (Specific, Measurable, Achievable, Relevant, Time-bound). This ensures that goals are clear, quantifiable, realistic, aligned with broader aspirations, and have a defined timeline for achievement.

5. **Prioritization**: Once SMART goals are established, collaboratively rank, or prioritize long-term goals based on their significance, impact, and feasibility. This helps ensure focus on the most critical objectives while creating a roadmap for phased achievement.

6. **Alignment with Values**: Now compare the prioritized SMART goals with the mentorship's long-term objectives ensuring they align with the mentee's core values and principles. Goals that resonate with the mentee's values are more likely to foster commitment and passion throughout the mentorship journey.

7. **Feedback and Refinement**: This is where working collaboratively comes to realization. You will work together soliciting feedback and challenging the long-term goals you have drafted. This is an iterative process allowing for refinement. You will challenge and scrutinize the draft goals repeatedly until you reach consensus that the long-term goals are agreed upon, realistic, and in the best interest of the mentee.

8. **Breakdown into Milestones**: Once feedback and refinement (above) have been completed, the mentor/mentee will collaboratively break down the long-term goals into smaller, manageable milestones. This facilitates a step-by-step approach, making the overarching goals more achievable and providing opportunities for celebration along the way.

9. **Resource Identification**: Develop further your plan for the long-term goals by identifying the resources, support, and guidance needed to accomplish the long-term goals. This may involve leveraging the mentor's network, budget approval, accessing specific training programs, or acquiring additional skills.

10. **Timeline Creation**: You are there. Develop a timeline for your plan that outlines the anticipated progression of achieving long-term goals. Remember to take into internal influences that may have an impact on the timeline such as company holidays, new product launches, and business travel, as well as, considering external influences such as vacations, holidays, and planned leaves of absence (LOA). This temporal structure helps both mentor and mentee stay on track and measure progress over time. Changes to the timeline should be agreed upon considering dependencies of one goal to another.

11. **Regular Evaluation and Adjustment**: Get things going and practice continuous assessment. Include in your plan regular evaluation and consideration for needed adjustments of long-term goals. This allows for flexibility in response to changing circumstances, emerging opportunities, or evolving priorities.

12. **Celebration of Milestones**: Do not forget the positive reinforcement! Celebrate the achievement of milestones within the long-term journey. Recognizing progress

reinforces commitment, boosts morale, and maintains motivation for the ongoing pursuit of overarching goals.

13. **Feedback Loop**: Include in your plans continuous feedback by establishing a continuous feedback loop between mentor and mentee. Regularly revisit long-term goals, assess progress, and adapt the plan based on evolving needs and circumstances.

Significance of Long-Term Goals:

1. **Visionary Direction**: Long-term goals provide a visionary direction, aligning the mentorship journey with the mentee's ultimate career and personal aspirations.

2. **Comprehensive Development**: Comprehensive long-term goals encompass various facets of personal and professional development, fostering a comprehensive approach to growth.

3. **Sustained Motivation**: The pursuit of long-term goals sustains motivation over the course of the mentorship, offering a continuous source of inspiration and purpose to the mentor and mentee.

4. **Increased Commitment**: Collaboratively defining and working toward long-term goals deepens the commitment of both mentor and mentee to the mentorship relationship.

5. **Building Resilience**: Long-term objectives necessitate resilience, adaptability, and perseverance, contributing to the mentee's overall resilience in the face of challenges.

6. **Continuous Learning**: The mentorship journey toward achieving long-term goals involves continuous learning, allowing the mentor/mentee to acquire new skills, insights, and perspectives. It is a win/win.

7. **Strategic Networking**: Long-term goals often involve strategic networking, exposing the mentee to valuable connections and opportunities within their chosen field.

8. **Culmination of Mentorship**: Achieving long-term goals marks the culmination of the mentorship journey, solidifying the mentor's/mentee's impact and growth.

Collaboratively defining ambitious yet attainable long-term goals in mentorship is a strategic process that provides a roadmap for sustained development. This approach ensures that the mentorship journey is purposeful, aligned with the mentee's overarching vision, and conducive to achieving meaningful, lasting outcomes.

B. Setting Realistic Expectations for Both Parties

Aligning Expectations: A Two-Way Street

Setting realistic expectations is foundational to a successful mentorship relationship, ensuring that both the mentor and mentee are on the same page regarding goals, communication, and the overall dynamics of their collaboration. Here are some strategies for mentors and mentees to align expectations and establish a shared understanding from the onset of the mentorship relationship:

Strategies for Mentors:

1. **Initial Expectation-Setting Meeting**: Time to roll up your sleeves and get this mentorship underway. The process for all mentorships will follow these same basic elements. The content will vary for each mentee since each mentee is a unique person and should be respected. Schedule a dedicated meeting early in the mentorship to begin to discuss expectations. Use this

meeting to clarify goals, establish communication preferences, and define the scope of the mentorship.

2. **Clearly Define Mentorship Goals**: Collaboration is an element used throughout mentorship. There will be times when each of you will work independently, but even that can be done in a collaborative spirit. Collaboratively identify and articulate specific mentorship goals. Clearly outline what each of you hopes to achieve and how you can support each other's aspirations. This process ensures alignment and mutual understanding.

3. **Discuss Availability and Communication Frequency**: Accept the reality that you will be dedicating time to mentorship. No worries, the upside is worth it. Establish expectations regarding availability and communication frequency. Discuss preferred modes of communication, response times, and how often mentor-mentee interactions should occur to avoid misunderstandings.

4. **Share Personal Mentorship Style**: Styles are as varied as people. It is important to note that mentorship styles are not mutually exclusive, and a mentor may incorporate elements from multiple styles based on the evolving needs of the mentee and the context of the mentorship relationship. Additionally, effective mentors are often adaptable and can adjust their style to best support the unique characteristics and goals of each mentee. Start by communicating your preferred mentorship style and approach – coaching style, advisory style, facilitative style, firsthand style, laissez-faire style, etc. This will help the mentees to define their style and needs, especially if they are new to mentorship.

5. **Highlight Areas of Expertise**: Make sure there is no misunderstanding on the part of the mentee by clearly outlining your areas of expertise and the support you

can provide. Ensure that the mentee understands the specific areas in which you can offer guidance, insights, and mentorship.

6. **Discuss Expectations Regarding Feedback**: Feedback is another essential component to mentorship. Without it there is uncertainty in the relationship between mentor/mentee. Set expectations around feedback, both positive and constructive. Clarify how feedback will be delivered, the frequency of feedback sessions (should be built into the plan, and the format (written, verbal, etc.). Written is recommended. **Feedback is not always positive, but it should always be delivered in a positive way**.

7. **Explain Boundaries and Limitations**: Boundaries or limitations are necessary. Communicate any boundaries or limitations you have as a mentor. Consider boundaries such as confidentiality, time commitments, professionalism, scope of expertise, personal space, feedback delivery, dependency, networking opportunities, personal gain, consistency in communication, gifts and favors, inclusion of others, and end of the mentorship. Be transparent and establish boundaries to manage expectations.

Strategies for Mentees:

1. **Reflect on Personal Goals**: You have been given a wonderful opportunity to receive direction and guidance from someone respected in your industry. Take it seriously and prepare for a rewarding and career advancing experience! You will start by reflecting on personal and professional goals before the mentorship begins. Come to the initial meeting prepared to discuss specific objectives, areas of growth, and what success looks like for you during and after the mentorship.

2. **Clearly Communicate Expectations**: Clarity is necessary. Considering your communications style and

skills, articulate your expectations clearly to the mentor in a manner that can be understood by them. Share what you hope to gain from the mentorship, including skills development, career guidance, and any specific challenges you are facing.

3. **Express Preferred Communication Style**: Related to the above, identify your communication styles. People often have a dominant style influenced by several factors such as personality, cultural background, and personal preferences. What is yours? Consider the following possibilities, assertive, passive, aggressive, passive-aggressive, analytical, intuitive , collaborative, directive, facilitative, expressive, precise, reflective. Communicate your preferred communication style and frequency. Let your mentor know how you prefer to communicate, whether it is through regular meetings, emails, or other means, to ensure alignment. Be open to your mentor's communication style and different communication styles.

4. **Ask About the Mentor's Availability**: You are both busy with the "daily routine." Inquire about the mentor's availability, limitations, and preferred response times. Understand when and how your mentor is available, ensuring realistic expectations and being respectful of their time commitments.

5. **Seek Clarification on Mentor's Expertise**: Do not be fooled by tenure, degrees, awards. Seek clarification on your mentor's areas of expertise. Ensure a clear understanding of your mentor's strengths, so you can align your expectations with their ability to provide guidance in specific areas.

6. **Discuss Feedback Preferences**: Feedback is an essential component to mentorship. It is coming so if you have "thin skin" spend some time setting expectations with your mentor. Set expectations around feedback, both positive and constructive. Clarify how

you prefer to receive feedback, the frequency of feedback sessions (should be built into the plan, and the format (written, verbal, etc.). Written is recommended. **Feedback is not always positive, but it should always be delivered in a positive way**.

7. **Understand Mentorship Dynamics**: Mentorship dynamics refer to the interactive and evolving relationship between a mentor and a mentee. This dynamic partnership involves a continuous exchange of knowledge, guidance, support, and feedback. The mentorship relationship is characterized by mutual respect, open communication, and a shared commitment to the mentee's personal and professional development. Key elements that define mentorship dynamics include, guidance and support, learning and development, two-way communication, goal setting and alignment, mutual respect and trust, adaptability and flexibility, skill transfer and knowledge sharing, feedback loop, empowerment and autonomy, networking and exposure, cultural sensitivity, and celebration of successes and achievements. This book will help you understand the roles of mentors and mentees and familiarize you with common mentorship practices.

Joint Strategies:

1. **Develop a Mentorship Agreement**: Your legal department is not needed for this, but a written mentorship agreement is strongly encouraged. This can be collaboratively created if your company does not have one. Draft a document that outlines mutual expectations, goals, and commitments. This agreement serves as a reference point throughout the mentorship. Like the mentorship plan it can be updated upon mutual agreement.

2. **Set SMART Goals** Establish SMART (Specific, Measurable, Achievable, Relevant, Time-bound) goals.

Collaboratively set goals that are realistic, measurable, and aligned with the overall objectives of the mentorship.

3. **Regular Check-Ins for Adjustments**: Schedule regular check-ins to discuss and adjust expectations. Unscheduled check-ins are helpful as well. These will occur when either party becomes aware of something that can impact the plan and it is best to share prior to the next scheduled check-in. Acknowledge that expectations may evolve, and plan regular opportunities to discuss and modify goals, communication strategies, and other aspects of the mentorship.

4. **Encourage Open Communication**: Open communication is a pillar to a successful mentorship journey. Mentor/mentee must always foster a culture of open communication. Both parties must endeavor to create an environment where both mentor and mentee feel comfortable expressing their expectations, concerns, and feedback.

5. **Provide Training on Effective Mentorship**: Learning about mentorship should be ongoing. This book is a good place to start. It offers strategies on effective mentorship practices. Organizations or mentorship programs can provide resources or workshops to educate both mentors and mentees on best practices, fostering a shared understanding of the mentorship process.

6. **Celebrate Milestones and Achievements**: Who does not like to celebrate successes especially when success was preceded by a lot of challenging work. Agree to celebrate achievements and milestones. Recognize and celebrate successes along the way, reinforcing the positive aspects of mentorship and maintaining motivation.

By implementing these strategies, mentors and mentees can establish a solid foundation for their mentorship relationship, ensuring that expectations are realistic, aligned, and conducive to a positive and fruitful collaboration. This initiative-taking approach sets the stage for a more effective and satisfying mentorship experience for both parties.

Managing Expectations Through Open Communication

Facilitating honest conversations about goals, time commitments, and the level of mentorship support is crucial for establishing a healthy and trusting dynamic between mentors and mentees. Open communication ensures that both parties are aligned in their expectations, leading to a more effective and satisfying mentorship experience. Here are some strategies to foster honest conversations:

Strategies for Mentors:

1. **Initiate a Goalsetting session**: Kick-off mentorship correctly by scheduling a dedicated session to collaboratively set goals. Actively listen to your mentee's concerns, ideas, and challenges they are facing or anticipate. It is so important to give them your full attention without interruption. Consider what they have shared, ask clarifying questions to verify your understanding so the goals are captured correctly. Having a documented plan sets the groundwork for managing expectations and avoiding confusion.

2. **Clarify Availability and Time Commitments**: Clearly communicate when, how often, how much time, and where will you meet. Share openly about availability and time constraints early on to manage expectations effectively.

3. **Share Your Mentorship Style**: We discussed mentorship styles briefly before. Let us delve deeper into some of those styles here. Remember, flexibility as you may need to adjust your style from one mentee to

the next. Which one are you? Here are some possibilities:

The Coach:

This mentor focuses on skill development and performance improvement. They provide specific guidance, feedback, and structured training to help the mentee acquire and refine specific skills.

The Advisor:

An advisor-style mentor offers expert advice and insights based on their own experiences. They serve as a source of wisdom and help mentees make informed decisions.

The Sponsor:

Sponsors actively advocate for their mentees within the organization. They help mentees access opportunities, connect with influential individuals, and navigate the corporate landscape.

The Role Model:

Role model mentors lead by example. They demonstrate behaviors, values, and work ethics that mentees can emulate. This style is particularly effective in shaping the mentee's professional identity.

The Facilitator:

Facilitator mentors empower mentees to take ownership of their development. They encourage self-directed learning, problem-solving, and decision-making, guiding mentees in finding their own solutions.

The Connector:

Connectors excel at expanding the mentee's network. They introduce mentees to valuable contacts, networking events, and opportunities to broaden their professional connections.

4. Establish Boundaries Clearly: Open communication suggests no boundaries, but boundaries in mentorship are essential to avoid confusion and clearly establish expectations. So be transparent about areas where you may not be able to provide support or expertise, fostering realistic expectations from the beginning. The mentee may need to seek mentorship from someone else that has expertise in those areas you lack.

5. Encourage Openness about Challenges: Ask powerful questions. Encourage the mentee to think critically and reflect on their experiences by asking open-ended questions. Here is an example, "What aspects of your current projects do you find most challenging and how do you think we can work together to address those challenges effectively?" Emphasize that it is okay for them to express difficulties or uncertainties, as addressing challenges is an integral part of the mentorship journey.

6. Set Expectations for Feedback: Feedback is part of open communication. Discuss the type and frequency of feedback the mentee can expect. Your mentorship and business style will come into play, but you must also consider the type of feedback the mentee is comfortable receiving. Establish clear expectations regarding feedback sessions, ensuring that both positive and constructive feedback are integral parts of the mentorship process.

7. Define Supportive Measures: There are a multitude of support measures that you can provide to the mentee. Share the support mechanisms you can provide. Consider the following as possibilities. You will see that each is an essential element of achieving open communication in mentorship.
- Active Listening
- Regular Check-ins
- Confidentiality
- Non-judgmental Attitude
- Empathy
- Feedback

- Encourage Questions
- Self-disclosure
- Empowerment
- Respect Difference
- Reflective Questions
- Patience
- Clarify Expectations
- Flexibility
- Follow-up

Strategies for Mentees:

1. **Share Your Mentorship Style:** Mentees can benefit from understanding different mentorship styles and how they align with their needs and goals. We presented above some of those styles the mentee may encounter. Mentees should assess their own preferences and goals to determine which mentorship style aligns best with their needs. Additionally, it is important to remember that mentors may use a combination of these styles, adapting to the mentee's evolving needs and circumstances.

2. **Express Personal and Professional Goals**: One of the first things you are going to collaboratively complete is a list of the mentorship goals. Articulate your personal and professional goals. Clearly communicate what you hope to achieve from the mentorship, ensuring that your mentor understands your expectations.

3. **Discuss Time Commitments**: Do not waste your time or that of the mentor. Discuss your availability and time constraints on an ongoing basis. Be honest about how much time you can dedicate to the mentorship, including meeting frequency, preparation, and follow-up commitments.

4. **Communicate Preferred Communication Style**: Share your preferred communication style. Communication styles may include any or a

combination of the following, open and direct, active listening, structured e.g. clear agendas, defined goals, and planned meetings), regular check-ins, flexible and informal conversations, feedback oriented, collaborative, and interactive, goal centric, and emotionally supportive. Which one do you prefer? Sharing your preference will help to align expectations.

5. **Seek Guidance on Mentor's Expertise**: This aligns with "establishing boundaries" for mentors (above). Inquire about your mentor's areas of expertise. Ask them to share with you those areas that they are comfortable providing support for and those for which you may need to seek mentorship elsewhere. Understand the specific areas in which your mentor can provide guidance to set realistic expectations about the scope of support.

6. **Discuss Learning Preferences**: Know and understand your learning preferences. These may include being a, visual learner, and auditory learner, a kinesthetic (learn through physical experiences), a reading/writing learner, a reflective (take your time and think deeply) learner, social learner, an independent learner, a sequential (step-by-step) learner, analytical learner, an emotional learner, or an experiential (learn best by doing) learner. Share how you prefer to learn and receive feedback.

7. **Ask About Mentorship Dynamics**: Mentorship dynamics refer to the interactive and evolving relationship between a mentor and a mentee. This dynamic partnership involves a continuous exchange of knowledge, guidance, support, and feedback. Inquire about your mentor's expectations regarding mentorship dynamics.

Understand your mentor's preferences for involvement and engagement to ensure a collaborative and satisfying mentorship experience. This may include:

- Asking questions and seeking clarification on any topic or advice provided by your mentor.
- Seeking feedback by requesting positive and constructive feedback on your performance and progress. Feedback is invaluable for your growth and improvement. Embrace constructive criticism.
- Reflect and apply what you have learned to your work and personal development.

8. **Be Grateful**: Express gratitude to your mentor for their time and guidance. Appreciation strengthens the mentorship relationship.

9. **Be Proactive**: Initiate communication with your mentor. Do not rely solely on them to set up meetings or discussions. Take the initiative to schedule check-ins and share updates.

Joint Strategies:

1. **Establish a Communication Plan**: Taking into consideration the communication style of the other, collaboratively create a communication plan. Do this by defining how often and through which channels you will communicate, ensuring that both mentors and mentees are comfortable with the chosen methods.

2. **Regularly Review and Adjust Expectations**: Include in your mentorship plan regular check-ins to review and adjust expectations. Do so with the understanding that expectations may evolve and change over time. Endeavor to create a culture of open communication where adjustments can be made as needed.

3. **Encourage Constructive Feedback**: Feedback goes both ways. Encourage feedback in two directions and foster an environment for constructive feedback. Do so by encouraging open discussions about the mentorship process, seeking feedback to continuously improve the

dynamic. **Feedback is not always positive, but it should always be delivered in a positive way**.

4. **Use Mentorship Agreements**: Under formal mentorship programs a Mentorship Agreement is a must-have. For less formal programs it is a clever idea to capture expectations and to avoid misunderstanding. Draft a mentorship agreement that outlines mutual expectations, goals, and commitments. This agreement serves as a reference point for both parties throughout the mentorship and is subject to change over time. Do not forget to capture the changes in the agreement. (See Appendices for a Mentorship Agreement template.)

5. **Establish a Safe Space for Honest Discussions**: Cultivate a safe space for honest conversations. The best time is during check-ins. Do so by ensuring that both parties to the relationship feel comfortable expressing their thoughts, concerns, and expectations without fear of judgment.

6. **Promote Flexibility**: In mentorship, "flexibility" refers to the mentor's/mentee's ability to adapt their approach, communication style, and guidance to meet the evolving needs, preferences, and circumstances of the mentorship relationship. Flexibility is a valuable quality in mentorship because it promotes trust and confidence. Here are some key aspects of flexibility in mentorship:

7. **Adapting to Learning Styles**: Flexibility means adjusting the mentorship approach to accommodate the varying learning styles and preferences of the mentor/mentee.

8. **Customizing Guidance**: Flexibility involves tailoring the mentor's guidance to the specific goals and challenges of the mentee. This may require mentors to provide diverse types of advice or resources based on the mentee's unique needs.

9. **Adjusting Communication**: Effective mentors/mentees are adaptable communicators. They can switch between formal and informal communication, adjust their tone, and use various communication channels (e.g., in-person meetings, email, video calls) based on what works best for the relationship.

10. **Recognizing Changing Circumstances**: Circumstances in a mentor's/mentee's life or career may change over time. Flexible mentors/mentees are responsive to these changes and are willing to revise goals, strategies, and plans as needed to ensure continued growth and development.

11. **Scheduling and Availability**: Flexibility also pertains to a mentor's/mentee's availability and willingness to accommodate the other person's schedule. This might involve scheduling meetings at convenient times or being open to last-minute discussions when urgent matters arise.

12. **Navigating Challenges**: Challenges and setbacks are a natural part of any mentorship journey. A flexible mentor/mentee will strive to be skilled at helping others navigate and overcome obstacles by adjusting strategies and providing emotional support when needed.

13. **Balancing Guidance and Autonomy**: Flexibility extends to the mentor's ability to strike the right balance between providing guidance and allowing the mentee to take ownership of their development. Mentors should adapt their level of involvement based on the mentee's readiness and capabilities.

14. **Embracing Diversity**: Mentors/mentees should be open to mentorship that is inclusive of individuals from diverse backgrounds, cultures, and experiences. Flexibility in understanding and respecting these differences is essential for effective mentorship.

15. **Feedback and Reflection**: Flexible mentors/mentees actively seek feedback from each other to gauge their satisfaction with the mentorship relationship. They are open to constructive criticism and are willing to reflect on their own mentoring practices to make improvements.

16. **Being Open to Change**: Flexibility in mentorship involves a willingness to embrace change and adapt to new circumstances, challenges, and opportunities. Emphasize flexibility in the mentorship relationship. Recognize that circumstances may change, and both parties should be open to adjusting expectations to accommodate evolving needs.

17. **Celebrate Successes and Milestones**: You will dedicate time and effort into mentorship so be available to celebrate achievements and milestones together. Positive reinforcement and celebration of successes contribute to a positive mentorship experience, motivating both mentors and mentees.

By implementing these strategies, mentors and mentees can create a foundation for open and honest communication, ensuring that expectations are aligned for a more effective and satisfying mentorship experience. This initiative-taking approach contributes to the development of a trusting and collaborative mentorship dynamic.

C. Creating a Mentorship Action Plan

An actionable mentorship plan provides a roadmap for the mentorship journey. In this section, mentors/mentees will explore the components of a comprehensive and effective action plan, including specific goals, timelines, and strategies for achieving milestones. Here are the key components for developing a comprehensive plan:

1. **Objective Identification**: Collaboratively, clearly define the objectives and goals of the mentorship relationship. First, the mentor and mentee should engage in an open dialogue to understand the mentee's aspirations, challenges, and areas of focus. The mentee should clearly communicate their short-term and long-term goals, whether it is career advancement, skill development, personal growth, or a combination. The mentor, using their skills and expertise can help the mentee refine their goals by using the SMART (specific, measurable, achievable, relevant, and time-bound) goal setting technique.

2. **Mentee's Development Needs**: During the goal setting process, the mentor can assess the mentee's current skills, knowledge, strengths, and areas for improvement. Identify the specific developmental needs that the mentorship will address.

Example:

A mentor is guiding a mentee through a career transition from a technical role to a leadership position within their organization. The mentor and mentee have identified potential challenges related to the transition, such as developing leadership skills, managing a team, and adapting to new responsibilities.

In this scenario, a known unknown could be the specific interpersonal challenges the mentee may encounter when managing a team. Both the mentor and mentee are aware that navigating team dynamics, resolving conflicts, and motivating team members will be part of the leadership role, but they do not have precise information about the individuals involved or the unique dynamics within the team.

To address this known unknown, the mentor and mentee could prepare by discussing general strategies for effective team leadership, conflict resolution techniques, and communication skills. They may also plan to address specific challenges as they arise, leveraging the mentor's experience and guidance.

While they are aware of the potential challenges in team management, the specific details and nuances are unknown until the mentee is actively in the leadership role.

3. **Resource Allocation**: Determine the resources required to support the mentorship plan. This may include access to training materials, workshops, networking opportunities, or specific tools needed for skill development.

4. **Feedback and Evaluation**: Establish a feedback loop where the mentor and mentee regularly evaluate progress toward goals and milestones. Feedback should be construc-tive and focused on growth. Discuss any adjustments needed to the plan.

Example:
Sarah M. is mentoring Alex K., a junior marketing professional looking to advance to a senior marketing role.
Together, they have set clear objectives, including Alex's
goal to lead a marketing campaign within the next six months.

The feedback loop they agreed upon after making their SMART goals included:
- **Regular check-ins:** Sarah and Alex scheduled bi-weekly meetings to discuss progress and any challenges. During these check-ins, they reviewed Alex's actions, discussed his experiences, and addressed any questions or roadblocks he encountered.
- **Milestone Assessment:** As Alex worked toward his goal, Sarah helped him break it down into smaller milestones. For instance, they identified

tasks such as conducting market research, developing a campaign strategy, and presenting it to the team as key milestones.

- **Feedback and reflection:** At each check-in, Sarah provided feedback on the quality of Alex's work, his leadership skills, and his ability to meet milestones. She offered constructive criticism and positive reinforcement to motivate him.
- **Adjustments and Adaptations**: If any challenges arose or if progress was slower than anticipated, Sarah and Alex discussed potential adjustments to the plan. They brainstormed solutions and adapted their approach accordingly.
- **Documentation**: Sarah and Alex kept a shared document outlining the goals, milestones, and progress made. This document served as a reference point during their discussions and allowed them to track achievements over time.
- **Celebrating Successes**: When Alex successfully led his first marketing campaign, Sarah and Alex took a moment to celebrate the achievement. This helped boost Alex's confidence and motivation.

This feedback loop in their mentorship relationship allowed Sarah and Alex to continuously evaluate progress, adapt to challenges, and celebrate achievements along the way.

5. **Support and Resources**: Ensure that the mentee has access to the necessary support and resources to achieve the mentorship goals. This could include introductions to relevant contacts, access to training programs, or mentorship-related materials.

6. **Conflict Resolution and Challenges**: Anticipate potential challenges or conflicts that may arise during the mentorship journey and outline strategies for addressing them. This may involve setting expectations for how to navigate disagreements or misalignments.

A comprehensive mentorship plan provides structure and clarity to the mentorship relationship, setting both mentor and mentee up for success. It allows for effective tracking of progress, adaptation to changing circumstances, and continuous improvement in achieving developmental goals. Regular communication and flexibility are essential to ensure that the plan remains relevant and aligned with the mentee's evolving needs and aspirations.

Customizing the Action Plan to Individual Needs

In this section, we discuss the importance of tailoring the mentorship action plan to the unique needs and aspirations of the mentee. Tailoring the mentorship action plan to the unique needs and aspirations of the mentee is of paramount importance for several reasons. It ensures that the mentorship journey is relevant, and meaningful, and directly contributes to the mentee's growth and development in a personalized and impactful way. Here is why this customization is crucial:

1. **Alignment with Individual Goals**: Discuss long-term goals and aspirations. Identify what the ultimate objective of the mentorship will be. Every mentee has specific career, personal, or skill development goals. Tailoring the mentorship action plan allows the mentor to address these unique objectives directly. When the plan aligns with the mentee's goals, it provides a clear path toward achieving them.

2. **Relevance and Motivation**: A personalized mentorship plan is highly relevant to the mentee's current situation and aspirations. This relevance is motivating for the mentee, as they can see how the mentorship journey directly applies to their needs and interests. It fuels their commitment to the process by allowing them to see a clear path toward their desired role.

3. **Focused Skill Development**: By customizing the plan, mentors can pinpoint the specific skills, knowledge, or competencies that the mentee needs to acquire or enhance. This focused approach ensures that the mentee's time and effort are directed toward areas that matter most. And the mentor can provide learning resources, recommended courses, and real-world examples that directly contribute to the mentee's skill development.

4. **Tailored Learning Styles**: Different mentees have different learning preferences. Some may learn best through firsthand experiences, while others prefer reading or one-on-one discussions. Customizing the plan allows the mentor to adapt their mentoring style to match the mentee's learning preferences. It also allows the mentor to incorporate practical exercises, shadowing opportunities and regular discussions about the nuances of the role the mentee desires to achieve.

5. **Maximizing Mentor's Expertise**: Mentors often have diverse expertise and experiences. Tailoring the plan allows mentors to leverage their own strengths and knowledge to best serve the mentee's needs. It ensures that the mentor's guidance is most relevant and valuable.

6. **Personalized Challenges and Growth Opportunities**: The mentorship action plan can include challenges and opportunities that are tailored to the mentee's unique circumstances. These challenges push the mentee out of their comfort zone in areas related to their growth and development. For example, a mentee struggles with public speaking and presenting to senior management. The mentor in response can integrate presentation skills coaching into their plan to help the mentee overcome this challenge.

7. **Measurable Progress**: Customized goals and action plans make it easier to measure progress by setting

clear, measurable milestones. The mentee can see tangible results and milestones, which provides a sense of accomplishment and reinforces the value of the mentorship journey. This may include achieving specific certifications, successfully managing a project, or presenting quarterly quality metrics to senior management.

To make the mentorship journey relevant, meaningful, and directly contributive to the mentee's growth and development, consider the following steps:

1. **Needs Assessment**: Begin by conducting a thorough needs assessment with the mentee. Understand their current skills, knowledge gaps, strengths, weaknesses, and career aspirations. Listen actively to their goals and challenges.

2. **Goal Setting**: Work collaboratively with the mentee to set clear and specific goals. These goals should be aligned with the mentee's aspirations and areas of improvement. Ensure that the goals are SMART (Specific, Measurable, Achievable, Relevant, Time-bound).

3. **Personalized Action Plan**: Develop an action plan that outlines the steps, tasks, and resources required to achieve the identified goals. Tailor the plan to match the mentee's learning style, pace, and preferences.

4. **Regular Check-Ins**: Schedule regular check-in meetings to monitor progress, discuss challenges, and make any necessary adjustments to the action plan. These meetings provide opportunities for ongoing customization.

5. **Feedback and Reflection**: Encourage the mentee to provide feedback on the mentorship journey and how well it aligns with their needs and aspirations. Use this feedback to refine and adapt the plan as needed.

6. **Flexibility**: Be flexible and open to changes in the plan as the mentee's circumstances or objectives evolve. A dynamic and adaptable approach ensures that the mentorship remains relevant.

7. **Celebrating Achievements**: Acknowledge and celebrate milestones and achievements along the way. Recognizing progress reinforces the mentee's commitment and motivation.

Example:

Your conversation will go something like this. The italicized words in parentheses are presented to show how the mentor and mentee are applying some of the skills presented in this chapter.

Mentor (Mark): Good morning, Sarah. I hope you are doing well today (*welcoming and creating a safe place*). I wanted to start our conversation by discussing our collaborative efforts for goal setting and needs assessment (*plan development and needs assessment*). How have you been since our last meeting?

Mentee (Sarah): Good morning, Mark. I have been doing well, thanks. I have been giving a lot of thought (*meeting preparation*) to our mentorship goals and where I see my-self in the future (*reflection*). I am excited to discuss how we can collaborate on setting those goals and identifying my needs (*enthusiasm*).

Mentor (Mark): That is great to hear (*supportive*), Sarah. It is crucial that we work together to define clear and meaningful goals for your mentorship journey (*collaboration and guidance*). What are some of the specific areas or objectives you would like to focus on during our time together?

Mentee (Sarah): Well, one of my main goals is to improve my leadership skills (*honesty and openness*). I

have been in a management role for a year now, and I
want to become a more effective leader. I would also like
to work on my project management abilities since that is a
big part of my current role (*identification of needed
skills*).

Mentor (Mark): Those are excellent goals, Sarah.
Leadership and project management skills are essential
for career growth (*supportive and feedback*). Let us dig a
bit deeper into each. What specific aspects of leadership
and project management do you think you would like to
enhance (*tailoring the plan*)?

Mentee (Sarah): For leadership, I would like to become
better at team motivation and conflict resolution. And in
terms of project management, I want to improve my
ability to set clear project goals and effectively allocate
resources (*honesty and skill specific*).

Mentor (Mark): That's very clear, Sarah (*positive and
support feedback*). To ensure our mentorship is tailored to
your needs (*Tailoring the mentorship plan*), I suggest we
break these down into SMART goals, which are Specific,
Measurable, Achievable, Relevant, and Time-bound. For
instance, we could set a SMART goal related to team
motivation within the next six months. How does that
sound to you (*collaborative*)?

Mentee (Sarah): That sounds like an excellent approach,
Mark (*feedback*). SMART goals will provide clear
direction, and I will be able to track my progress
effectively (*restating understanding of plan*).

Mentor (Mark): Great! In addition to setting goals, we
should also assess your current skills and identify areas
where you need additional support or development (*plan
development and needs assessment*). This will help us
create a comprehensive plan. How would you like to
proceed with the skills assessment (*seeking
collaboration*)?

Mentee (Sarah): I think a self-assessment, followed by a discussion with you, would be beneficial (*honesty and expressing need*). It will allow me to reflect on my strengths and weaknesses, and your insights can help me gain a more objective perspective (*milestone*).

Mentor (Mark): That is a good plan, Sarah (*positive feed back*). Let us start with a self-assessment, and we will schedule a meeting to review your findings. This collaborative effort in setting clear goals and assessing your needs will form the foundation of our mentorship journey, ensuring it is tailored to your growth and development.

Customizing the mentorship action plan is a collaborative effort between the mentor and mentee. When done effectively, it transforms the mentorship journey into a highly personalized, impactful, and fulfilling experience that directly contributes to the mentee's growth and development.

D. The Importance of Regular Check-ins and Feedback

Regular check-ins and feedback are vital components of a dynamic mentorship relationship, playing a pivotal role in its success. These practices foster an environment of continuous improvement, open communication, and mutual growth. First, regular check-ins provide structured opportunities for the mentor and mentee to assess progress, discuss challenges, and align their efforts toward shared goals. This ongoing dialogue ensures that the mentorship remains on track, relevant, and responsive to the evolving needs and aspirations of the mentee.

Furthermore, feedback is a powerful tool that fuels personal and professional development. It offers valuable insights into strengths, areas for improvement, and opportunities for growth. In a mentorship relationship, feedback flows in both directions, allowing the mentor to provide constructive guidance and the mentee to offer insights on the mentorship process itself. This reciprocal feedback loop builds trust, strengthens the mentorship bond, and accelerates the learning curve for the mentee. Regular check-ins and feedback transform mentorship into a dynamic, adaptive, and enriching journey that maximizes the potential for growth and success.

Building a Cadence of Communication

Regular check-ins form the backbone of a dynamic mentorship relationship. In this section, mentors/mentees will understand the significance of establishing a consistent communication cadence, allowing for real-time feedback, updates on progress, and addressing any emerging challenges for several reasons:

1. **Real-time Feedback and Guidance**: Regular check-ins create a structured platform for mentors/mentees to provide timely feedback to each other. This real-time feedback is invaluable as it allows mentees to make immediate adjustments and improvements in their actions, decisions, and skill development. It prevents small issues from escalating into larger problems and ensures that the mentor's guidance is relevant to the mentee's current circumstances.

   Example:
   A mentee might say, "I've been struggling with time management and consistently missing project deadlines. Would it be possible to schedule a session where we can work together to identify strategies to improve my time management skills?"

2. **Progress Tracking**: Consistent communication enables mentors and mentees to track progress toward established goals and milestones. It provides a clear picture of what has been achieved and what remains to be done. This tracking is essential for maintaining motivation, celebrating achievements, and identifying

areas where additional support or effort may be required.

3. **Adaptation to Changing Needs**: Over the course of a mentorship relationship, goals and challenges may evolve because they are not static. They evolve due to changing aspirations, skill development, external factors, feedback, and life events. A flexible and adaptable mentorship plan allows for these shifts. To stay on track, regular check-ins allow both parties to stay informed about these changes. This adaptability ensures that the mentorship plan remains aligned with the mentee's current priorities, enhancing its relevance and effectiveness.

4. **Building Trust and Rapport**: Frequent communication builds trust and rapport between mentors and mentees. It fosters a sense of connection and commitment to the mentorship relationship. Mentees are more likely to seek guidance and share their concerns when they have regular interactions with their mentors. Mentors can demonstrate trustworthiness by actively listening to their mentees' concerns, questions, and aspirations. They should show genuine empathy and understanding of the mentee's perspective using active listening.

    Example:
    You may want to initiate a conversation about trust and rapport at the beginning of the mentorship relationship. Discuss your expectations, goals, communication preferences, and the importance of confidentiality. This open and transparent dialogue sets the foundation for a trusting and productive mentorship relationship.

5. **Problem-Solving**: Challenges and obstacles are natural in any developmental journey. Regular check-ins provide a forum for mentees to discuss emerging challenges with their mentors. This problem-solving

dialogue needs to be open and direct to allow mentors to offer insights, strategies, and resources to help mentees overcome obstacles more effectively.

Example:
During a scheduled check-in, a mentee might say, "I've encountered a challenge in managing my team's dynamics. Some conflicts have arisen, and it is affecting our productivity. I wanted to discuss potential strategies to address this issue and would appreciate your insights."

6. **Continuous Learning**: Both mentors and mentees benefit from ongoing learning through regular communication. Mentors can gain insights into the evolving needs and perspectives of the newer generation, while mentees can learn from the experiences and wisdom of their mentors. This reciprocal learning enriches the mentorship experience.

   Example:
   Engage in regular communication to plan progress, challenges, and learning experiences. Share a specific situation from work and encourage one another to reflect on strategies and areas for improvement. This continuous dialogue allows for ongoing learning and skill development in a supportive mentorship relationship.

7. **Accountability**: Regular check-ins create a sense of accountability for both mentors and mentees. Knowing that there are scheduled meetings encourages both parties to stay committed to their mentorship goals and responsibilities. This accountability helps maintain momentum and progress.

8. **Efficiency**: A consistent communication cadence helps optimize the use of time and resources. It ensures that mentor-mentee interactions are purposeful and

productive, as discussions are focused on addressing immediate needs, challenges, and goals.

In summary, the significance of establishing a consistent communication cadence in a mentorship relationship cannot be overstated. It facilitates real-time feedback, progress tracking, adaptation to changing needs, trust-building, problem-solving, continuous learning, accountability, and efficiency. These benefits collectively contribute to the success and impact of the mentorship journey, ensuring that both mentors and mentees achieve their desired outcomes and growth.

The Transformative Power of Feedback

Feedback is a catalyst for growth. In this section, mentors/mentees will gain insights into delivering constructive feedback in a safe and comfortable environment is crucial for motivating and guiding the mentee toward improvement while fostering a reciprocal learning experience for the mentor. Here are some insights on how to achieve this:

1. **Create a Supportive Atmosphere**: Start by establishing a positive and supportive atmosphere in your mentorship relationship. Ensure that the mentee feels valued and respected. Emphasize that feedback is a tool for growth, not criticism.

2. **Use a Balance of Positive and Constructive Feedback**: A balanced approach to feedback combining both positive and constructive feedback is advocated. Ken Blanchard, co-author of the "One minute Manager"[13], emphasizes the importance of providing clear and balanced feedback. Douglas Stone and Sheila Heen, authors of "Thanks for the Feedback: The Science and Art of Receiving Feedback Well" explore various aspects of feedback, including the importance of balancing positive and negative feedback.[14]

   The "sandwich technique"[13] or sandwich approach to providing feedback involves sandwiching constructive feedback between positive feedback or praise. The idea is to provide feedback in a way that begins and ends on a positive note, with constructive feedback placed in the middle. This approach to providing feedback has gotten mixed reviews. It is less effective in certain situations because of lack of clarity because the recipient may focus more on the positive than the constructive comments. It should be delivered genuinely, or it may come across as being insincere.

3. **Be Specific and Actionable**: Feedback should be specific and actionable. Instead of vague statements like "You need to improve communication," provide concrete examples and suggestions. For instance, "I noticed during our last meeting that you had some difficulty articulating your ideas. To improve, you could try summarizing your key points before sharing them."

4. **Focus on Behavior, Not Personality**: Frame feedback around observable behaviors or actions, not the mentee's personality or character. This helps the mentee understand that improvement is attainable through changes in behavior. For example, say, "I observed that in team meetings, you tend to interrupt others. Consider actively listening and waiting for others to finish before speaking."

4. **Ask for Permission**: Before providing feedback, ask the mentee if they are open to receiving it. This approach allows the mentee to mentally prepare and signals your respect for their autonomy. Say something like, "Would you be open to some feedback on your recent presentation?"

5. **Encourage Self-Reflection**: Encourage the mentee to engage in self-reflection by asking open-ended questions like, "How do you think that meeting went?" This allows the mentee to assess their performance and identify areas for improvement independently.

6. **Offer Guidance, Not Solutions**: Instead of dictating solutions, guide the mentee toward finding their own solutions and strategies for improvement. This approach empowers the mentee to take ownership of their growth. Ask questions like, "What do you think might help you address this challenge?"

5. **Be Sensitive to Timing**: Choose the right moment to provide feedback. Avoid addressing sensitive issues in high-stress situations or in front of others. Find a private and comfortable setting where the mentee can absorb the feedback without feeling defensive.

6. **Active Listening**: After delivering feedback, actively listen to the mentee's response. Give them the opportunity to share their perspective, thoughts, and feelings. This fosters a two-way dialogue and demonstrates that you value their input.

7. **Follow Up and Track Progress**: Regularly follow up on the feedback provided and track the mentee's progress. Celebrate improvements and discuss any challenges or setbacks. This ongoing dialogue ensures that feedback remains a continuous part of the mentorship journey.

8. **Be Open to Receiving Feedback**: Encourage the mentee to provide feedback on your mentoring style and guidance. This reciprocal feedback allows both mentor and mentee to learn from each other's perspectives and contributes to mutual growth.

By delivering constructive feedback in a safe and comfortable environment using these strategies, mentors/mentees can motivate and guide one another toward improvement while fostering a reciprocal learning experience. This approach promotes trust, transparency, and a growth-oriented mindset within the mentorship relationship.

Putting It All Together: A Case Study

To illustrate the principles discussed in this chapter, we present a real-world case study highlighting a mentorship journey that successfully implemented clear goals, managed expectations, created an actionable plan, and prioritized regular check-ins and feedback.

Case Study: A Transformative Mentorship Journey
Mentor: Malcolm L.
Mentee: John C.

Background:

Malcolm L., a seasoned executive with over three decades of experience in the medical device, pharmaceutical, and health care data analysis industry, recognized the potential for mentorship to nurture talent within his organization. He volunteered to mentor John C., a bright and ambitious recent college graduate he just hired, with no experience in any regulated industry. John aspired to begin his career and was eager to learn from Malcolm's wealth of knowledge and leadership skills.

Setting Clear Goals:

The mentorship journey began with a clear definition of goals. Together, Malcolm and John identified and documented John's short-term and long-term objectives. John aimed to become an operations manager of a small medical device manufacturing company within a year and eventually the head of all operations. Malcolm helped John articulate these goals into SMART (Specific, Measurable, Achievable, Relevant, Time-bound) targets.

Managing Expectations:

One of the initial discussions revolved around managing expectations. Malcolm emphasized that mentorship was a partnership, with responsibilities for both mentor and mentee. They established that John would actively seek guidance, proactively implement feedback, and come prepared for each meeting. Malcolm, on the other hand, is committed to offering guidance, sharing experiences, and providing constructive feedback. He made it clear that his availability was limited.

Creating an Actionable Plan:
Malcolm and John developed a mentorship action plan based on John's goals. The plan included specific tasks and milestones, such as setting up the manufacturing facility, writing procedures, hiring, training, and managing the first employees, attending leadership workshops, and hosting client and regulatory audits. They tailored the plan to John's learning style, incorporating firsthand experiences, reading assignments, and one-on-one discussions.

Prioritizing Regular Check-Ins and Feedback:
To ensure consistent progress, Malcolm and John scheduled bi-weekly check-in meetings. During these sessions, they reviewed completed tasks, discussed challenges, and celebrated achievements. Feedback was central to their mentorship journey. Malcolm provided specific, actionable feedback on John's writing, communication skills, and project management. John, in turn, offered feedback on Malcolm's mentoring approach, fostering a culture of reciprocal learning.

Key Milestones:
Six months into the mentorship, John successfully led a cross-functional project, demonstrating his leadership abilities.

At the one-year mark, John was promoted to operations manager, aligning with his short-term goal.

Malcolm and John continued their mentorship beyond the initial year, adapting the goals to John's evolving career aspirations.

Outcome:
John's mentorship journey with Malcolm was a resounding success. He not only achieved his short-term goal but also continued to grow as a leader. The tailored mentorship

plan, consistent feedback, and ongoing support from Malcolm empowered John to realize his potential. The mentorship relationship evolved into a lifelong connection, with John now serving as a mentor to the plant manager, QA/QC Managers, Regulatory Manager, and the Facilities Manager within the organization.

This case study highlights the power of clear goals, managed expectations, an actionable plan, and regular check-ins and feedback in a mentorship journey. It demonstrates how a resolute mentor like Malcolm can make a lasting impact on a mentee's career and personal development.

In conclusion, in Chapter 4 we learned that mastering the art of mentorship begins with the meticulous establishment of clear goals and expectations. By defining objectives, aligning expectations, creating a comprehensive action plan, and prioritizing regular communication and feedback, mentors and mentees can lay the groundwork for a transformative and purposeful mentorship journey.

List of Chapter 4 Highpoints:

- Distinguish between short-term and long-term goals within the mentorship, ensuring that both mentor and mentee have an unclouded vision of immediate and future objectives.
- Setting realistic expectations for both mentor and mentee is crucial to avoid misunderstandings and ensure a successful relationship.
- Create a detailed mentorship action plan, which includes specific steps, milestones, and timelines to achieve the set goals.
- Mentors/mentees MUST calendar regular check-ins to monitor progress, address challenges, and make necessary adjustments to the mentorship plan.

- Clear communication about each party's expectations and boundaries is needed to foster a respectful and productive mentorship relationship.

Call to Action for the Mentor:

1. Assist your mentee in setting both short-term and long-term goals. Ensure that these goals are SMART (Specific, Measurable, Achievable, Relevant, Time-bound).
2. Define and communicate your boundaries and availability to your mentee to set realistic expectations about the mentorship.
3. Collaborate with your mentee to develop a structured action plan that outlines steps to achieve the identified goals.
4. Schedule and conduct regular check-ins to review progress, provide feedback, and make any necessary adjustments to the action plan.
5. Foster an environment where your mentee feels comfortable sharing their thoughts, challenges, and successes.

Call to Action for the Mentee:

1. Clearly articulate your short-term and long-term goals for the mentorship and share them with your mentor.
2. Recognize and respect the role and boundaries of your mentor, understanding that their guidance complements but does not replace your own effort.
3. Actively participate in creating the mentorship action plan, taking responsibility for your part in executing it.
4. Come prepared to regular check-ins with updates on your progress, questions, and feedback.
5. Take initiative in your learning and development and maintain open lines of communication with your mentor.

Chapter Five: Effective Communication in Mentorship

Mastering effective communication is the linchpin of successful mentorship. In this chapter, we will delve into the art and science of communication, exploring strategies for active listening, providing constructive feedback, navigating difficult conversations, and leveraging technology to enhance remote mentorship.

A. Active Listening and Open Communication

The Power of Active Listening

Active listening is the cornerstone of effective communication. Mentors and mentees will explore the art of fully engaging in conversations, demonstrating empathy, and seeking to understand before being understood. Practical techniques for active listening will be discussed to enhance the quality of mentorship interactions.

Active listening is a characteristic of empathic listening and is a communication skill that encompasses a range of techniques and behaviors designed to enhance understanding and demonstrate attentiveness when engaged in a conversation. It involves fully focusing on and comprehending what the speaker is saying, both verbally and non-verbally. Here are some key elements of active listening:

1. **Giving Full Attention**: Active listening requires the listener to give their undivided attention to the speaker. This means avoiding distractions, such as checking phones or thinking about unrelated matters.

   Example:
   Christina is mentoring John. During a mentorship meeting, Christina encourages John to open up about

some difficulties meeting project timelines. As John begins to share, Christina puts her phone in silence mode and places it face down on her desk, ensuring no distractions. Making eye contact with John, she tells him, "Please go ahead and share more about these challenges. I'm here to listen."

In this example, Christina demonstrates giving her full attention to John by putting her phone on silent and placing it face down on her desk. This action shows that she is fully engaged in the conversation and prioritizes active listening. She also reassures John that she is there to listen, creating a safe and open space for him to share his challenges and concerns.

2. **Maintaining Eye Contact**: Making eye contact with the speaker can sometimes be difficult but shows that you are engaged and interested in what they are saying. However, it is essential to do so without making the speaker uncomfortable. Here are three ways that will help to prevent making the speaker uncomfortable:

   A. **The 50/70 Rule**: Instead of rigidly staring into the speaker's eyes, which can be intimidating, use the 50/70 rule. This means making eye contact about 50% of the time while speaking and increasing it to around 70% while listening. This approach strikes a balance between engagement and not making the speaker feel scrutinized.

   B. **Soften Your Gaze**: When maintaining eye contact, soften your gaze by focusing on the speaker's eyes and occasionally shifting your gaze to their face as a whole. Avoid locking onto one eye or staring intensely, which can be unsettling. The goal is to convey warmth and interest rather than intensity.

   C. **Blink and Look Away Naturally**: Blinking is a natural part of eye contact. Allow yourself to blink regularly, and when you need to break eye contact briefly, do so naturally. Look away momentarily, such as to glance at notes or nod in acknowledgment. This provides small breaks in eye contact without appearing disinterested.

Remember that cultural norms and individual preferences can influence how eye contact is perceived, so it is essential to be adaptable and responsive to the speaker's cues. The goal is to create a comfortable and engaged listening environment.

3. **Using Verbal and Non-Verbal Cues**: Nodding, smiling, and using verbal affirmations like "I see," "I understand," or "Tell me more" can encourage the speaker to continue sharing their thoughts and feelings. While verbal and nonverbal cues are essential components of active listening, they have their limitations. Here are some limitations for using verbal and non-verbal cues during active listening:

    A. **Cultural Differences**: Verbal and non-verbal cues can be interpreted differently across cultures. What may be considered a positive cue in one culture could be seen as disrespectful or inappropriate in another. It is essential to be aware of cultural norms and adapt your cues accordingly when communicating with individuals from iverse cultural backgrounds. Talk about the possibility of cultural differences to avoid any miscommunication!

    B. **Misinterpretation**: Both verbal and non-verbal cues can be misinterpreted. For example, a nod of the head or saying "yes" might indicate agreement or understanding in one context but merely acknowledgment in another. Misinterpreting cues can lead to misunderstandings and breakdowns in communication. The context in which these cues are used needs to be considered at the time of communication.

    C. **Inconsistent Signals**: Sometimes, verbal, and non-verbal cues can send conflicting signals. For instance, a person may verbally express agreement but display nonverbal cues of disagreement, such as crossed arms or a furrowed brow. In such cases, it is crucial to seek clarification to understand the true message. If either party is uncertain about verbal and non-verbal cues seek clarification by paraphrasing your understanding.

D. **Overuse or Fakeness**: Overusing certain cues or using them inauthentically can undermine trust and rapport. For example, excessive nodding or smiling without genuine engagement can come across as insincere or patronizing. Authenticity is key to effective communication.

E. **Assumptions**: Relying solely on non-verbal cues can lead to assumptions about the speaker's emotions or intentions. For instance, assuming that someone is angry based on their facial expression without confirming their feelings through verbal communication can be misleading.

F. **Individual Differences**: People have varying communication styles and preferences. Some individuals may be less expressive with their non-verbal cues or have different patterns of using verbal cues. It is essential to adapt your listening approach to accommodate these individual differences and to discuss communication styles early in the mentorship relationship.

G. **Limited Context**: Verbal and non-verbal cues provide context to the conversation, but they may not always provide the full picture. Without additional information, it can be challenging to understand the deeper motivations or emotions behind the speaker's words and actions.

H. **Mood and Stress**: A person's mood or stress level can impact their use of verbal and non-verbal cues. For example, someone experiencing high stress may not display typical cues, making it challenging to gauge their true emotions or receptiveness. Beware of your emotional state and its potential impact on communication. It may be better to postpone a planned discussion if mood or stress may prevent effective communication.

To mitigate these limitations, effective active listening requires a comprehensive approach that combines verbal and non-verbal cues with other elements such as asking open-ended questions, paraphrasing, and seeking clarification when necessary. It is also important to remain attentive and adaptable to the specific context and the individual you are communicating with.

4. **Paraphrasing**: Active listeners often summarize or paraphrase what the speaker has said to confirm understanding and show that they are following the conversation. Here are 3 suggestions for active listeners when paraphrasing:

   1. **Use Reflective Statements**: Instead of simply repeating the speaker's words verbatim, use reflective statements to capture the essence of what they have said.

      Example:

      Mentee: "I've been working long hours to meet project deadlines."
      Mentor (Active Listener): "So, you've been putting in extra hours to ensure the project stays on track."

      Reflective statements rephrase the speaker's message in your words while maintaining the core meaning.

   2. **Ask Clarifying Questions**: After paraphrasing, follow up with a clarifying question to confirm your understanding and encourage the speaker to provide more details.

      Example:

      Mentee: "I've been feeling overwhelmed with my

responsibilities."
Mentor (Active Listener) (after paraphrasing): "It sounds like you're dealing with a lot. Can you tell me more about the specific challenges you are facing?"

Asking clarifying questions not only shows your interest but also ensures that you are comprehending the speaker's perspective accurately.

C. **Validate Emotions**: In addition to paraphrasing the content, acknowledge and validate the speaker's emotions or feelings. This demonstrates empathy and a deeper level of understanding.

Example:
Mentee: "I'm frustrated because I can't seem to resolve these issues."
Mentor (Active Listener) (after paraphrasing): "I can hear your frustration. It must be challenging when you're dealing with these unresolved issues."

Validating emotions shows that you are attuned to the speaker's emotional state and that you care about how they are feeling.

These suggestions help create a supportive and engaging conversation environment by confirming your comprehension of the speaker's message and encouraging them to share more. Remember that paraphrasing should be done genuinely and without overuse to maintain a natural flow in the conversation.

5. **Avoiding Interruptions**: It is crucial not to interrupt the speaker while they are talking. Let them finish their thoughts before responding. Here are 3 additional suggestions for active listeners to avoid interrupting the speaker:

A. **Use Non-Verbal Cues**: Employ non-verbal cues to signal your intent to listen without interruption. Maintain eye contact, nod in acknowledgment, and maintain an open and attentive posture. These cues convey that you are fully engaged and receptive to the speaker's words.
B. **Practice Patience**: Cultivate patience during the conversation. Embrace moments of silence, as they can indicate that the speaker is collecting their thoughts or preparing to share something important. Resist the urge to fill these pauses with your own input.
C. **Wait for Natural Pauses**: Instead of interrupting mid-sentence, wait for natural pauses in the speaker's speech, such as when they take a breath or complete a thought. This allows you to interject at a point that feels less disruptive and respects the speaker's flow.

These strategies help you demonstrate active listening while minimizing interruptions, which can disrupt the speaker's train of thought and hinder effective communication.

6. **Asking Open-Ended Questions**: Open-ended questions encourage the speaker to provide more information and insights. These questions typically start with words like "how," "what," "why," and "tell me about." Here are two examples:

Example 1:
Mentor: "Tell me about your long-term career aspirations and how you envision achieving them."

This open-ended question invites the mentee to share their career goals and the strategies they have considered for reaching those goals. It encourages the mentee to express their thoughts and aspirations in detail, fostering a deeper and more meaningful conversation.

Example 2:
Mentor: "Can you describe a recent challenge you've faced in your work or studies? What steps have you taken to address it, and what have you learned from the experience?"

This question prompts the mentee to discuss a specific challenge they have encountered, the actions they have taken to overcome it, and the insights gained from the process. It not only allows the mentee to reflect on their experiences but also provides an opportunity for the mentor to offer guidance and support based on the mentee's response.

Both open-ended questions encourage the mentee to share their thoughts, experiences, and perspectives while allowing the mentor to actively listen and provide relevant guidance or feedback.

7. **Empathizing**: Demonstrating empathy involves understanding and acknowledging the speaker's feelings, even if you do not necessarily agree with their perspective. Here are 3 suggestions for the listener in such situations:

   A. **Acknowledge the Emotions**: Focus on the speaker's emotions rather than their viewpoint. Express understanding and empathy for how they feel without necessarily agreeing with their position. For example:

      Listener: "I can see that you're really frustrated about this situation, and that's completely valid. I appreciate you sharing your perspective."

By acknowledging their emotions, you validate their feelings and show that you are attentive to their emotional state.

B. **Ask Open-Ended Questions**: Encourage the speaker to share more about their perspective by asking open-ended questions that delve deeper into their thoughts and feelings. For example:

Listener: "I understand that you see it that way. Can you help me understand more about what led you to this viewpoint?"

This approach allows the speaker to elaborate on their perspective and provides an opportunity for a more comprehensive and empathetic conversation.

C. **Respect Differences**: Acknowledge that it is okay to have differing viewpoints. You can express your respect for their perspective even if you do not agree with it. For example:

Listener: "While I may see this differently, I respect your viewpoint and value our ability to have an open and honest conversation."

This statement emphasizes the importance of respectful dialogue and maintains a positive and empathetic tone in the conversation.

Demonstrating empathy, especially in disagreement, helps maintain a constructive and supportive dialogue, even when perspectives diverge. It fosters a sense of mutual respect and understanding, which is essential in mentorship and communication in general.

8. **Avoiding Judgment**: Active listening requires suspend-ing judgment and refraining from evaluating or criticizing the speaker's thoughts or opinions. Here are

3 suggestions for the listener to avoid the appearance of being judgmental:

A. Acknowledge the Emotions: Focus on the speaker's emotions rather than their viewpoint. Express understanding and empathy for how they feel without necessarily agreeing with their position. For example:

Listener: "I can see that you're really frustrated about this
situation, and that's completely valid. I appreciate you
sharing your perspective."

By acknowledging their emotions, you validate their feelings and show that you are attentive to their emotional state.

B. Ask Open-Ended Questions: Encourage the speaker to share more about their perspective by asking open-ended questions that delve deeper into their thoughts and feelings. For example:

Listener: "I understand that you see it that way. Can you help me understand more about what led you to this viewpoint?"

This approach allows the speaker to elaborate on their perspective and provides an opportunity for a more comprehensive and empathetic conversation.

C. Respect Differences: Acknowledge that it is okay to have differing viewpoints. You can express your respect for their perspective even if you do not agree with it. For example:

Listener: "While I may see this differently, I respect your viewpoint and value our ability to have an open and honest conversation."

This statement emphasizes the importance of respectful dialogue and maintains a positive and empathetic tone in the conversation.

Demonstrating empathy, especially in disagreement, helps maintain a constructive and supportive dialogue, even when perspectives diverge. It fosters a sense of mutual respect and understanding, which is essential in mentorship and communication in general.

9. **Reflecting Emotions**: Acknowledging and reflecting the speaker's emotions can help them feel heard and understood. For example, saying, "It sounds like you're feeling frustrated" demonstrates empathy.

    Example:

    Mentee: "I've been working on this project tirelessly, but it seems like my efforts are going unnoticed."
    Mentor: "I can sense that you're investing a lot of time and dedication into this project, and it's important to you that your contributions are recognized."

    In this example, the mentor acknowledges and reflects the mentee's emotions of feeling undervalued and unheard without using the specific phrase "It sounds like you are feeling frustrated." Instead, the mentor uses a different approach to convey understanding and empathy for the mentee's situation. This demonstrates active listening and a willingness to support the mentee's concerns.

10. **Summarizing and Clarifying**: Periodically summarizing what has been discussed and asking for clarification when something is unclear can ensure that both parties are on the same page. See below additional guidance on summarizing and clarifying.

11. **Resisting the Urge to Provide Solutions Immediately**: In some cases, the speaker may not

wantadvice or solutions right away. Active listening involves respecting their need to express themselves before moving to problem-solving. Here are 3 suggestions for the listener in such situations:

A. **Reflective Responses**: Instead of jumping to solutions, the active listener can offer reflective responses that encourage the mentee to explore their own thoughts and solutions.

    Example:

    Mentee: "I'm not sure how to handle this conflict with my team."
    Active Listener: "It sounds like you're facing a challenging situation with your team. What are some approaches you have considered for resolving the conflict?"

By posing this question, the active listener prompts the mentee to think critically about potential solutions before offering their own input.

B. **Socratic Questioning**: Active listeners can use Socratic questioning[14] techniques to guide the mentee in problem-solving. This involves asking open ended questions to encourage critical thinking, reflection, and problem solving that lead the mentee to analyze a particular issue and generate ideas independently.

    Example:

    Mentee: "I'm struggling to prioritize my tasks effectively."
    Active Listener: "What factors do you think are contributing to the difficulty in prioritization? Can you identify any patterns or areas where you would like to improve?"

Socratic questioning helps the mentee gain insight into their challenges and fosters a sense of ownership over the solutions.

C. **Summarization and Exploration**: Instead of immediately proposing solutions, the active listener can summarize the mentee's concerns and encourage further exploration.

Example:

Mentee: "I'm unsure about which career path to pursue."
Active Listener: "I hear you're at a crossroads in your career. Can you tell me more about your interests, values, and what excites you about different career options?"

By asking for more information and insights, the active listener assists the mentee in examining their options more deeply and making informed decisions.

These approaches allow the active listener to support the mentee in finding their own solutions and empower them to take ownership of their challenges, which is a valuable aspect of mentorship.

Active listening is a fundamental skill in effective communication, whether in personal or professional relationships. It helps build trust, enhances understanding, and fosters stronger connections between individuals.

Fostering Open Communication

Openness sets the stage for honest and transparent communication. In this section mentors/mentees will learn how to create an environment where both feel comfortable sharing their thoughts, concerns, and aspirations. Here are some strategies for both parties:

Strategies for Mentors:

1. **Lead by Example**: Mentors can set the tone by being open, sharing their experiences (including challenges and mistakes), and demonstrating vulnerability. When mentees see their mentors being open, they are more likely to reciprocate.

   Example:

   Scenario: Maureen is a seasoned sales executive mentoring Petr, a junior salesperson in a formal mentorship relationship.

   Maureen: "Petr, let me share an experience from early in my career that taught me the importance of adaptability. When I was in your shoes, I was assigned to lead a major project, and I was confident it would be a tremendous success. However, as things unfolded, unexpected challenges arose, and the project did not go as planned. It was a difficult period for me because I had to admit my mistakes and ask for help from my colleagues and supervisor."

   Petr: "Wow, Maureen, I wouldn't have expected you to face setbacks like that."

   Maureen: "Absolutely, and that's the point. We all encounter challenges and make mistakes. What is important is how we learn from them and grow. I had to be open about my struggles, ask for guidance, and work collaboratively with my team to turn things around. It was a valuable lesson in adaptability and resilience."

In this example, Maureen leads by example by sharing a personal story that highlights her own challenges and mistakes. By doing so, she demonstrates vulnerability and shows Petr that even experienced professionals face difficulties. This encourages openness and trust in the mentorship relationship, making it easier for Petr to share his own challenges and seek guidance.

2. **Active Listening**: Mentors should actively listen to mentees without judgment and provide a safe space for them to express their thoughts and concerns. This helps mentees feel heard and valued.

3. **Build Trust Gradually**: Trust is the foundation of openness. Mentors should work on building trust incrementally, ensuring that mentees feel comfortable sharing their thoughts and fears over time.

4. **Encourage Questions**: Mentors can invite questions and curiosity by emphasizing that there are no "silly" or "wrong" questions. This encourages mentees to seek clarification and express themselves openly.

Strategies for Mentees:

1. **Express Your Goals and Expectations**: At the beginning of the mentorship relationship, mentees can openly discuss their goals, expectations, and what they hope to gain from the mentorship. This sets clear intentions and fosters transparency.

2. **Share Challenges**: Mentees should feel comfortable sharing challenges, uncertainties, and areas where they need guidance. Being open about difficulties allows mentors to provide targeted support.

3. **Seek Feedback Actively**: Actively request feedback from your mentor on your progress, performance, and areas for improvement. This demonstrates a willingness to learn and grow.

4. **Acknowledge Mistakes**: When mentees make mistakes or encounter setbacks, they should be open about them rather than trying to hide or downplay them. This openness can lead to valuable learning experiences.

Example:

Scenario: David is a mentee in a mentorship program, and he has been working with his mentor, Bridget, who is an experienced project manager.

David: "Bridget, I wanted to talk to you about a recent project I was managing. I made a significant mistake in the planning phase that caused delays and budget overruns. I initially felt embarrassed and didn't want to admit my error, but I realized that hiding it wouldn't help anyone."

Bridget: "Thank you for sharing that, David. Making mistakes is a part of our professional journey. Can you tell me more about what happened?"

David: "Certainly. I underestimated the complexity of a particular task and did not allocate enough resources for it. It resulted in missed deadlines and increased costs. However, I learned a valuable lesson about the importance of thorough planning and resource allocation. I've already taken steps to rectify the situation and ensure it doesn't happen again."

Bridget: "That's a great attitude, David. We all make mistakes, but the key is to learn from them. In fact, I had a similar experience early in my career, and it taught me the importance of meticulous project planning. It's great that you're applying this lesson proactively."

In this example, David acknowledges his mistake openly with his mentor, Bridget. By doing so, he not only demonstrates honesty but also creates an opportunity for a valuable learning experience. Bridget, in turn, shares her own experience, emphasizing that making mistakes is a part of professional growth. This open and honest exchange contributes to David's development as he learns from the mistake and takes steps to improve his project management skills.

5. **Clarify Expectations**: If mentees have questions or concerns about the mentorship process or the mentor's guidance, they should openly communicate these and seek clarification. Clearing up misunderstandings ensures a productive relationship.

6. **Express Gratitude**: Mentees can openly express gratitude for their mentor's support and guidance. This fosters a positive and appreciative atmosphere in the mentorship.

By implementing these strategies, mentors and mentees can cultivate a culture of openness and transparent communication, which, in turn, leads to a more effective and fulfilling mentorship relationship.

B. Providing Constructive Feedback

The Purpose of Constructive Feedback

Constructive feedback is a catalyst for growth. In this section mentors/mentees will understand the importance of providing feedback that is specific, actionable, and focused on improvement. We will discuss the transformative power of constructive feedback in shaping mentors'/mentees' skills and behaviors.

Strategies for Mentors:

1. **Create a Safe Environment**: Ensure that the feedback process takes place in a safe and supportive environment where the mentee feels comfortable discussing areas for improvement without fear of judgment. A safe environment is one where the mentorship includes:

A. **One-on-One Meetings**: Meetings held every other Monday in a quiet office or conference room where the sessions are dedicated to discussing the mentee's progress, challenges, and goals. Active listening, constructive feedback, and sharing of relevant experiences occurs.

B. **Customized Learning Plan**: A personalized learning plan developed collaboratively and tailored to the mentee's career aspiration is used. The plan is specific and progress toward achieving milestones is assessed.

C. **Open Door Policy**: Time is set aside allowing the mentee to feel comfortable approaching the mentor outside of scheduled meetings for advice or to discuss urgent matters.

D. **Encouraging Independence**: The mentee is encouraged to apply new skills and think independently while completing tasks that gradually increase in complexity.

E. **Respectful and Inclusive Language**: Both parties use language that is respectful and inclusive, while avoiding any language that could be construed as discriminatory or offensive.

F. **Recognition of Achievements**: The mentor acknowledges the mentee's achievements through verbal praise, written commendations, public recognition, certificates or awards, company points/dollars (if available), professional development opportunities, and increased responsibilities as a few examples.

G. **Feedback Mechanism**: Company mentorship programs should include periodic (monthly) anonymous feedback where both parties can express their thoughts about the program. In less formal programs, the parties can speak openly to one another about the program. Both approaches ensure continuous improvement.

H. **Emotional Support and Encouragement**: During challenging times e.g., a mistake of failure, either party offers emotional support and encouragement.

1. **Adjustments as Needed**: As the mentorship matures, both parties will recognize the need to adjust the level of support and guidance offered. This will allow the mentor-ship to remain relevant and effective.

In this environment, the mentee feels supported, valued, and empowered to develop professionally, while also feeling comfortable to express concerns and ask for help.

2. **Be Specific**: Offer specific examples and details to illustrate your feedback. Avoid vague statements and provide concrete instances where the behavior or performance could be improved.

Example:

Scenario: The mentee has recently completed a feature for the web application, which allows users to upload and manage documents. However, the feature has some performance issues and lacks certain user-friendly elements.

Mentor's Specific Feedback: "I reviewed the document upload feature you implemented for the web application. I appreciate your effort in getting it functional ahead of schedule. However, I have noticed a couple of areas where it can be improved:

Performance Issue: When I tested the feature with multiple files, the upload speed significantly slowed down after the fifth file. This is an issue in how the uploads are being handled. I recommend optimizing the file handling logic. What are your thoughts?

User Interface Enhancement: The current design lacks a progress bar or any indication for users to know the status of their uploads. Adding a visual cue, like a progress bar or a notification upon completion, would enhance user experience.

Testing Recommendation: Ensure to include more comprehensive tests, particularly for uploading large files or different file formats. This will help catch any potential bugs and improve the robustness of the feature.

Action Plan: "Let's schedule a pair programming session next week to work on the performance optimization together. I can share some techniques that might be helpful."

"For the User Interface improvement, you might want to look into some existing progress bar implementations or libraries that we can integrate."

In this example, the mentor's feedback is specific and directly addresses aspects of the mentee's work. The mentor acknowledges the mentee's efforts and successes but also provides clear guidance on areas for improvement, along with suggestions and an action plan to help the mentee enhance their skills and the project outcome.

3. **Focus on Behavior and Impact**: Concentrate on the mentee's actions, behaviors, or work outcomes rather than making personal judgments or assumptions about their character or intentions. Describe the impact of their actions on projects, colleagues, or company goals.

4. **Offer Solutions or Suggestions**: Alongside pointing out areas for improvement, provide constructive suggestions or potential solutions. Help the mentee understand how to address the identified issues. See scenario provided above.

5. **Use a Balance of Positive and Constructive Feedback**: There are many thoughts on providing feedback. A balanced approach to feedback combining both positive and constructive feedback is advocated. Regardless of the method employed, it should be delivered genuinely, or it may come across as being insincere.

Strategies for Mentees:

1. **Be Open to Feedback**: Mentees should approach feedback with an open and receptive mindset. Understand that feedback is a valuable opportunity for growth and improvement. Here are some suggestions to demonstrate you have an open and receptive mindset to feedback:

    A. **Active Listening**: When receiving feedback, the mentee should listen attentively, making eye contact and nodding to show they are engaged. They should avoid interrupting the mentor and allow them to fully express their thoughts.

    B. **Asking Clarifying Questions**: If any part of the feedback is unclear, the mentee should ask questions for clarification. This shows that they are interested in understanding the feedback fully and are keen on applying it correctly.

    C. **Acknowledging the Feedback**: The mentee can acknowledge the feedback received by summarizing the main points. For example, "So, to make sure I understand, you're suggesting I should focus more on optimizing the code for better performance."

    D. **Expressing Gratitude**: A simple "thank you for the feedback" demonstrates appreciation for the mentor's efforts in providing guidance. It shows that the mentee values the mentor's input and time.

    E. **Reflecting on the Feedback**: The mentee can take time to reflect on the feedback and consider how it applies to their work. This reflection can be shared with the mentor later, showing that they have taken the feedback seriously.

    F. **Discussing Implementation Plans**: The mentee can discuss how they plan to implement the feedback, asking for suggestions if needed. This initiative-taking approach shows they are eager to improve.

G. Showing Improvement: Apply the feedback in your work and show improvement over time is the most effective way to demonstrate a receptive mindset. It shows the mentor that their advice has been heeded and valued.

H. Open Body Language: Maintaining an open and engaged body posture during feedback sessions (like uncrossed arms, facing the mentor) non-verbally communicates receptiveness.

I. Regular Updates: The mentee can provide the mentor with regular updates on their progress, especially concerning areas where feedback was given. This keeps the mentor informed and shows the mentee's commitment to growth.

J. Seeking Additional Feedback: The mentee can actively seek out additional feedback, indicating their ongoing commitment to self-improvement and valuing the mentor's perspective.

K. Sharing Challenges and Successes: Being open about challenges they face in implementing the feedback and sharing successes when they manage to overcome these challenges.

By engaging in these behaviors, a mentee can effectively communicate to their mentor that they are open and receptive to feedback, fostering a productive and positive mentor-mentee relationship.

2. **Ask for Clarification**: If the feedback is unclear or you need further information to understand it better, do not hesitate to ask your mentor for clarification. Seek examples and specifics.

3. **Avoid Defensive Responses**: Instead of becoming defensive when receiving feedback, focus on active listening and understanding the mentor's perspective. Avoid the urge to justify or explain your actions immediately. Here are some examples of such responses and why they should be avoided:

A. **Immediate Justifications**: Responding with immediate justifications for your actions or decisions, such as "I did it this way because...", can come across as if you are not open to considering other perspectives or acknowledging potential areas for improvement.

B. **Denial of the Issue**: Outright denying that there is a problem or an area needing improvement, for example, saying "No, that's not right" or "That's not a problem," can be perceived as being closed-minded or unwilling to accept constructive criticism.

C. **Blaming Others**: Shifting the blame to others, such as team members or external circumstances, with responses like "It wasn't my fault, the team didn't..." can indicate an unwillingness to take responsibility for one's own contributions or mistakes.

D. **Making Excuses**: Offering excuses rather than addressing the feedback, for example saying, "I was really busy with other tasks, so I couldn't..." This can be seen as evading accountability.

E. **Questioning the Mentor's Credibility**: Challenging the mentor's knowledge or expertise by saying things like "Are you sure that's the best way to do it?" or "I think my method is better," can damage the trust and respect in the mentor-mentee relationship.

F. **Overreacting Emotionally**: Displaying strong emotional reactions, such as anger or frustration, can be counterproductive. For instance, showing visible annoyance or saying, "This is so unfair," suggests an inability to handle feedback maturely.

G. **Interrupting the Mentor**: Cutting off the mentor while they are still giving feedback with responses like "Let me explain why I did that," can come across as disrespectful and impatient.

H. **Ignoring the Feedback**: Showing a lack of interest or indifference, such as not engaging in the conversation or not making eye contact, can be interpreted as ignoring the value of the feedback.

I.   Overgeneralizing the Feedback: Responses like "I always mess things up" or "I can never get this right" can indicate a defeatist attitude and an inability to see feedback as an opportunity for specific improvement rather than a general personal failure.

J.   Sarcasm or Mocking: Responding with sarcasm or mocking the feedback, even if in jest, can be perceived as disrespectful and a sign of not taking the feedback seriously.

Avoiding these defensive responses is crucial for a mentee. Instead, they should aim to demonstrate openness, willingness to learn, and respect for the mentor's perspective. This approach not only fosters personal growth but also strengthens the mentor-mentee relationship.

4.   **Reflect and Plan**: Take time to reflect on the feedback you receive. Consider how you can apply the feedback to improve your performance or behavior. Create an action plan for implementing changes.

5.   **Seek Regular Feedback**: Encourage ongoing feedback discussions with your mentor. Do not wait for formal feedback sessions; ask for feedback regularly to ensure continuous improvement.

6.   **Express Appreciation**: After receiving feedback, express your gratitude to your mentor for their guidance and insights. This reinforces a positive and appreciative atmosphere. Consider the following ways to sincerely express appreciation for feedback:

   A.   Verbal Acknowledgment: Be polite! A simple, direct statement can be highly effective. After receiving feedback, the mentee can say something like, "Thank you for this feedback. I really appreciate your insights and the time you have taken to help me improve." This not only shows gratitude but also acknowledges the mentor's effort and expertise.

B. **Follow-Up Email or Note**: Sending a follow-up email or a handwritten note expressing thanks can be a thoughtful gesture. The mentee could write something like, "I have been reflecting on the feedback you gave me, and I wanted to express my gratitude. Your advice is incredibly valuable to my professional growth, and I am thankful for your guidance and support." This provides a tangible record of appreciation and shows the mentor that their feedback has been taken seriously.

C. **Implementing Feedback and Sharing Results**: One of the sincerest ways to show appreciation is by putting the feedback into action. The mentee can later share with the mentor how the feedback was implemented and the positive outcomes that resulted. For instance, "I applied the strategies you suggested in my last project, and it made a significant difference in the outcome. Thank you for pointing me in the right direction." This not only shows gratitude but also demonstrates the mentee's commitment to growth and learning.

These actions help to reinforce a positive mentor-mentee relationship, fostering an environment of mutual respect and continuous learning.

Remember that constructive feedback is a two-way street in mentorship. Both mentors and mentees play a role in ensuring that the feedback process is constructive, supportive, and conducive to growth and development.

The Art of Positive Criticism

In this section, mentors-mentees will learn the art of delivering criticism in a way that motivates and inspires rather than demoralizes. Techniques for framing feedback positively and providing actionable steps for improvement are provided, fostering a constructive and supportive mentorship environment.

Here are some strategies and techniques:

1. **Start with Positives**: Begin the feedback conversation with praise or acknowledgment of the mentor's/mentee's strengths and achievements. This sets a positive tone for the discussion and helps the mentor/mentee feel valued.

2. **Focus on Behavior, Not Personality**: Ensure that your feedback addresses specific behaviors, actions, or outcomes rather than making judgments about the mentor's/mentee's personality or character. This helps keep the feedback constructive and actionable.

3. **Use the "I" Statement**: Frame feedback using "I" statements to express your perspective without sounding accusatory. For example, say, "I noticed that in the last meeting, your presentation lacked some key details," instead of "You didn't include important details in your presentation."

4. **Be Specific and Concrete**: Provide specific examples of the behavior or performance you are addressing. Avoid vague or generalized feedback, as it can be unclear and less actionable.

5. **Offer Solutions or Suggestions**: Alongside pointing out areas for improvement, provide constructive suggestions or potential solutions. Help the mentee understand how to address the identified issues.

6. **Use a Balance of Positive and Constructive Feedback:"** A balanced approach to feedback combining both positive and constructive feedback is advocated

7. **Highlight Growth Potential**: Emphasize that feedback is an opportunity for growth and development, not a judgment of the mentee's worth. Discuss how making

improvements can contribute to their personal and professional advancement.

8. **Encourage Self-Reflection**: Encourage the mentor/mentee to reflect on the feedback and consider how they can apply it to their development. Ask open-ended questions like, "How do you think you can work on this aspect?"

9. **Set Clear and Achievable Goals**: Collaboratively establish clear and achievable goals based on the feedback. Ensure these goals are specific, measurable, and time-bound (SMART).

10. **Provide Ongoing Support**: Offer your ongoing support and guidance as you work on improving. Let each other know you are there to help and provide resources or assistance as needed.

11. **Monitor Progress**: Regularly check in with each other to monitor your progress and provide additional feedback, as necessary. Celebrate milestones and achievements along the way.

12. **Maintain a Growth Mindset**: Foster a growth mindset in the mentorship relationship by emphasizing that mistakes and setbacks are opportunities for learning and improvement, not failures.

Remember that the key to delivering positive criticism is to strike a balance between offering constructive feedback and maintaining a supportive and encouraging mentorship environment. By using these strategies, mentors can inspire mentees to embrace feedback as a pathway to growth and success.

C. Navigating Difficult Conversations

Recognizing the Need for Difficult Conversations

Difficult conversations are inevitable in any mentorship journey. In this section mentors/mentees will explore how to recognize when a difficult conversation is necessary and strategies for approaching these discussions with sensitivity and clarity. Here are some strategies for mentors/mentees for maintaining a positive mentorship relationship through difficult conversations.

Recognizing the Need for Difficult Conversations:

1. **Notice Patterns**: When you observe recurring issues or challenges that hinder the mentee's progress, it may be an indication that a difficult conversation is needed. These patterns could include has not shown much interest in the mentorship or skill in accomplishing tasks that part of the plan, missed deadlines, consistent errors, mistakes are made and no interest in fixing it for themselves, not engaged in the mentorship, missed meetings, or consistently requests postponement, or interpersonal conflicts.

2. **Trust Your Gut**: If you have a gut feeling that something is amiss or that there is an underlying issue affecting the mentee's performance or well-being, it is worth exploring through a conversation.

3. **Feedback Is Ignored**: If you have provided feedback or guidance multiple times on a particular issue, and there is little to no improvement, it may be time for a more in-depth conversation.

Approaching Difficult Conversations:
- **Choose the Right Time and Place**: Find a suitable, private, and comfortable setting for the conversation. Ensure that both you and the mentee

have enough time to discuss the issue without feeling rushed.

- **Get Into the Right Mindset**: If you feel uncomfortable having a difficult conversation, you can "coach" yourself into a mindset that will make you feel more confident. Before the conversation, organize your thoughts and gather relevant information or examples. Consider what you want to achieve from the conversation and how you can convey your message. Go somewhere private or close your office door and talk yourself into the right mindset. Coaching questions may include:
- Why are you delaying this conversation?
- Will delaying make the issue go away?
- How will the mentor-mentee be helped by having this conversation?
- What reaction do you anticipate and how can you prepare to deal with the reaction?
- How will this conversation make you feel and how will you deal with that, so you are not distracted from what you need to do?
- What is the right thing to do? Remember you are this person's mentor/mentee.
- What is the goal of having this conversation?
- Are there any benefits of doing it right now?

3. **Use "I" Statements**: Frame your feedback using "I" statements to express your perspective without sounding accusatory. For example, say, "I've noticed that there have been consistent issues with meeting on time," instead of "You always miss our mentorship meeting start times."

4. **Active Listening**: Give the mentee an opportunity to express their thoughts and feelings. Actively listen without interrupting and use paraphrasing to confirm your understanding of their perspective.

5. **Ask Open-Ended Questions**: Encourage the mentee to share their thoughts and ideas by asking open-ended

questions. For example, "Can you tell me more about your perspective on this issue?"

6. **Stay Calm and Non-Judgmental**: Maintain a calm and non-judgmental demeanor throughout the conversation. Avoid blame or making assumptions about the mentor's-mentee's intentions.

7. **Empathize and Validate**: Show empathy and understanding for the mentor's/mentee's perspective, even if you disagree. Validating their feelings can help build trust and rapport.

8. **Focus on Solutions**: Collaboratively explore potential solutions or strategies for improvement. Encourage the mentor-mentee to be an active participant in finding solutions.

9. **Agree on Action Steps**: Ensure that the conversation results in actionable steps and a plan for moving forward. Clearly define what changes or improvements are expected and establish timelines.

10. **Follow Up**: Schedule follow-up meetings to track progress, offer additional support, and provide positive reinforcement for improvements.

Remember that difficult conversations, when handled sensitively and with clear communication, can lead to resolution, growth, and stronger mentorship relationships. Mentors/mentees should approach these conversations with a shared commitment to mutual understanding and improvement.

Example:

Scenario: A mentor, Anne, needs to have a difficult conversation with their mentee, Justine, who is a junior graphic designer. Justine has been consistently missing project deadlines, impacting the team's workflow.

Anne (Mentor) using a calm and conversational manner: "Justine, I appreciate you taking the time to meet with me today. I want to talk about a critical issue that has been affecting our team's workflow (*impact of behavior*). I have noticed that the last few projects you have been involved in have been submitted past their deadlines (*clear statement of situation*). Meeting deadlines is crucial in our line of work to maintain client satisfaction and team efficiency (*expected behavior*). Can you share your perspective on what has been happening?" (*Asking for mentee's perspective*)

Justine (Mentee) while Anne listens politely: "I understand. I've been feeling overwhelmed with the workload and have had trouble managing my time effectively."

Anne (encouraging openness and paraphrasing): "Thank you for sharing that, Justine. It is important to communicate if you are feeling overwhelmed so we can find a solution together. One approach could be to improve time management skills (*generating solutions*). For instance, breaking down projects into smaller tasks with individual deadlines might help. What do you think about this, or do you have other solutions in mind?" (*Seeking collaboration and agreement on solutions*)

Justine: "Breaking down projects does sound helpful. Maybe I could also benefit from some additional training on the latest design software to speed up my workflow."

Anne: "That's a great idea. Let us set up a plan where you break down your next project into smaller tasks. Also, I will arrange for a training session on the new software. We can check in weekly to discuss your progress and adjust as needed. How does that sound?"

Justine: "That sounds really helpful. I think these steps could improve my performance."

Anne: "Excellent. I will summarize our plan: You will start breaking down projects into smaller tasks, and we will schedule training for you on the new software. We will have weekly check-ins to monitor your progress. Remember, I believe in your abilities and am here to support you. We all face challenges, and it's how we overcome them that matters."

Justine: "Thank you, Anne. I appreciate your support and guidance."

Anne: "Of course. Let us schedule our first check-in for next Friday. I'm confident that with these adjustments, you'll be able to meet your deadlines more consistently."

In this conversation, Anne effectively initiates the difficult conversation by stating the issue clearly and expressing the expectation (meeting deadlines). Anne invites Justine to share their perspective, listens actively, and collaborates on generating solutions. They agree on a specific action plan, summarize the steps Justine will take, reiterate their belief in Justine's ability to improve, and schedule a follow-up to assess progress. This approach ensures that the conversation is constructive, supportive, and focused on positive change.

Techniques for Successful Navigation

In this section mentors-mentees will see how the practical techniques presented above and for navigating difficult conversations presented in this section, including active listening, empathetic communication, and problem-solving, can be used to gain insights into turning challenges into opportunities for growth within the mentorship relationship. Techniques for navigating difficult conversations include:

1. **Open Communication**: By fostering open and honest communication, mentors and mentees can identify challenges early and discuss them openly. This allows for a deeper understanding of the underlying issues and provides an opportunity to explore potential solutions.

2. **Active Listening**: Active listening helps mentors/mentees better understand each other's perspectives, including the challenges they face. This empathetic approach can lead to insights into the mentorship relationship's needs, mentee's aspirations, and areas requiring development.

3. **Collaborative Problem-Solving**: Engaging in difficult conversations often leads to the co-creation of solutions. Mentors/mentees can brainstorm and work together to address challenges, turning them into actionable strategies for growth.

4. **Setting Clear Goals**: During difficult conversations, mentors/mentees can define clear goals for improvement. These goals become opportunities for growth and achieving them can lead to a sense of accomplishment and development.

5. **Feedback and Reflection**: Feedback provided during difficult conversations can serve as a valuable source of insights. By reflecting on feedback and considering how to apply it, mentors/mentees can identify areas where they can grow and enhance their skills.

6. **Learning from Mistakes**: Difficult conversations may involve discussing mistakes or setbacks. Embracing these as learning experiences can lead to personal and professional growth. Mentors can guide mentees in extracting lessons from their challenges.

7. **Resilience Building**: Resilience in a mentorship relationship is about building a solid foundation that allows both mentor and mentee to thrive in the face of challenges, constantly learning, and growing together. Facing and addressing challenges can contribute to the development of resilience. Mentors can help mentees view challenges as opportunities to build resilience, adaptability, and problem-solving skills.

Some key aspects of resilience in a mentorship relationship include:

- Facing Challenges Together
- Learning from Failure
- Adapting to Change
- Maintaining a Positive Outlook
- Providing Emotional Support
- Encouraging Self-care and Balance
- Celebrating Progress/Successes
- Building Critical Thinking Skills
- Continuous Learning and Growth
- Modeling Resilient Behavior

8. **Continuous Improvement**: By consistently addressing challenges and seeking opportunities for improvement, mentors-mentees cultivate a culture of continuous learning and growth within their mentorship relationship.

In summary, the techniques outlined above, such as open communication, active listening, and collaborative problem-solving, can help mentors/mentees gain valuable insights into how challenges can be transformed into opportunities for personal and professional growth through open communication. This initiative-taking and constructive approach contributes to a more rewarding and impactful mentorship journey.

D. Leveraging Technology for Remote Mentorship

The Rise of Remote Mentorship

The increase in remote mentorship is a direct consequence of the larger shift towards remote work, a trend accelerated by global events. This transition to virtual environments has transformed traditional mentorship models, offering unique advantages and challenges. In this section mentors/mentees will explore the advantages and challenges of remote mentorship. We will discuss how technology can bridge the gap and enhance mentorship connections regardless of geographical distances.

One significant advantage of remote mentorship is the expansion of accessibility. Mentors and mentees are no longer constrained by geographic limitations, allowing for more diverse pairings and the sharing of a wider range of experiences and skills. Additionally, the flexibility in scheduling that comes with remote work can make it easier to arrange mentorship sessions, accommodating varied time zones and work-life commitments. The use of digital tools—such as video conferencing, collaborative platforms, and instant messaging enhances the immediacy and convenience of communication, allowing for more frequent and versatile interactions.

However, these benefits come with their own set of challenges. Building rapport and trust, which are critical components of successful mentorship, can be more difficult in a remote setting. The absence of face-to-face interaction means non-verbal cues are often lost, potentially leading to misunderstandings or a sense of disconnect. Furthermore, the reliance on technology introduces the risk of technical issues, which can disrupt the flow of communication. Another challenge is the potential for decreased engagement or commitment, as the informal, spontaneous interactions that occur in physical workspaces are absent in remote settings. Both mentors and mentees may need to put extra effort into maintaining engagement and ensuring that the mentorship remains a priority.

While remote mentorship offers the advantages of increased accessibility and flexibility, it requires careful navigation of communication challenges and a concerted effort to maintain engagement and build a strong, trusting relationship. The success of remote mentorship hinges on the ability of both parties to adapt to these new dynamics and fully leverage the digital tools at their disposal.

Tools and Platforms for Remote Mentorship

Mentors and mentees will gain insights into various tools and platforms that facilitate remote mentorship, from video conferencing to collaboration tools. Practical tips for leveraging technology to maintain a strong mentorship connection will be provided.

The landscape of remote mentorship is supported by a diverse array of tools and platforms, each catering to distinct aspects of the mentoring process. Video conferencing tools like Zoom, Microsoft Teams, and Google Meet have become staples for face-to-face interactions. They facilitate real-time communication and help in mimicking the in-person meeting experience. For more informal or quick exchanges, messaging platforms such as Slack, WhatsApp, or Microsoft Teams offer a convenient way to stay in touch, share updates, and provide timely feedback.

Beyond these, there are specialized mentorship platforms like MentorCruise, Ten Thousand Coffees, and Chronus, which are specifically designed to facilitate mentor-mentee connections. These platforms often come with features like matching algorithms to pair mentors and mentees based on specific criteria, tracking progress over time, and providing resources for learning and development. For sharing documents, giving feedback on work, and collaborative project management, tools like Google Drive, Dropbox, Trello, and Asana are invaluable. They allow for seamless collaboration and ensure that mentor/mentee have easy access to relevant materials.

For successful application of these tools in maintaining a strong mentorship connection, several strategies can be employed. The reader will note that these strategies align with those presented for successful mentorship.

1. **Establish Clear Communication Protocols**: At the start of the mentorship, agree on which tools to use for different purposes. For instance, decide to use email for

formal communication, instant messaging apps for quick queries, and video conferencing for in-depth discussions. Set expectations about response times and availability to avoid misunderstandings.

2. **Regular Scheduled Meetings**: Utilize video conferencing tools like Zoom or Microsoft Teams for regular, scheduled meetings. These should be consistent (e.g., weekly, or bi-weekly) and planned in advance to maintain a rhythm in the mentorship. The visual aspect of video calls helps in building rapport and facilitates more personal and engaging conversations.

3. **Leverage Collaborative Tools for Shared Projects**: For any collaborative work, use platforms like Google Drive or Trello. These tools can be used to track progress on specific projects or goals, share resources, and provide feedback. It is important to regularly update and review these platforms to keep both parties engaged and on track.

4. **Utilize Specialized Mentorship Platforms**: If using platforms designed specifically for mentorship, like MentorCruise or Chronus, take full advantage of their features. These might include mentor-mentee matching, goal setting and tracking, and accessing educational resources. These platforms can provide structure and additional resources to enhance the mentorship experience.

5. **Encourage Open and Continuous Communication**: Outside of scheduled meetings, encourage regular communication through messaging platforms. This keeps the dialogue open and allows for timely advice or feedback. It is important to create an atmosphere where the mentee feels comfortable reaching out with questions or updates at any time.

6. **Goal Setting and Progress Tracking**: Use digital tools to set clear goals and track progress. This could involve

creating shared documents or spreadsheets where both mentor and mentee can note objectives, deadlines, and accomplishments. Regularly review these goals during meetings to assess progress and adjust as needed.

7. **Feedback Mechanisms**: Incorporate regular feedback sessions into the mentorship. This can be done through video calls or written evaluations. Feedback should be constructive, focusing on areas of improvement and acknowledging achievements.

8. **Adapt and Be Flexible**: Be prepared to adapt the use of tools and strategies as the mentorship relationship evolves. Flexibility is key in remote settings as needs and circumstances can change.

9. **Personal Touch**: Despite the digital nature of interaction, strive to maintain an individualized touch. Celebrate achievements, acknowledge personal milestones, and show genuine interest and care in the mentee's professional and personal development.

10. **Encourage Self-Directed Learning**: Use digital platforms to provide resources for further learning. This could include sharing articles, online courses, webinars, etc., which can be discussed later in mentorship sessions.

By strategically applying these tools and strategies, the mentorship relationship can thrive in a remote environment, providing an effective and fulfilling experience for both mentor and mentee.

Case Study: Application of Strategies
To illustrate the principles discussed in this chapter, we will present a case study highlighting effective communication in mentorship. This example will highlight the successful application of active listening, constructive feedback, handling difficult conversations, and leveraging technology for remote mentorship.

Cast Study #1 – Nonremote, Client Services Case Study
Mentor: Tina R.
Mentee: Natalia R.

Background:

In a bustling client services firm, "A+ Customer Experience", a mentorship program was initiated to foster professional growth among junior employees. Tina R., a seasoned Client Services Sr. Manager with over a decade of experience, was paired with Natalia R., a recent college graduate who had just joined the firm as a Client Services Associate.

The Beginning: Establishing the Relationship

Tina and Natalia's mentorship kicked off with an in-person meeting in a quiet conference room at the firm. Tina, aware of the importance of active listening, encouraged Natalia to share her career aspirations, challenges she anticipated, and her initial impressions of the workplace. Tina attentively listened, acknowledging Natalia's enthusiasm and apprehensions, and established a foundation of trust and open communication.

Leveraging Technology

To effectively manage their mentorship journey, Tina introduced Natalia to the firm's internal project management tool. They used this platform to set goals, track progress, and schedule regular meetings. Tina also showed Natalia how to use client relationship management software, crucial for their roles, enhancing Natalia's technical skills and confidence in managing client data.

Midway: Handling Difficult Conversations

A few months into the mentorship, Tina noticed that Natalia was struggling with managing demanding clients, which occasionally led to missed deadlines. Tina initiated a difficult conversation, first acknowledging Natalia's hard work and then delicately addressing the issue. She provided specific examples of where improvements could be made and asked Natalia for her perspective.

Natalia felt comfortable enough to admit her struggle with
time management when dealing with challenging client
requests. Tina appreciated her honesty and they worked
together to develop strategies for better time management and
client communication.

Constructive Feedback

Tina regularly provided Natalia with constructive feedback.
She praised Natalia's dedication and quick learning but also
pointed out areas for improvement, like her approach to client
follow-ups and report accuracy. Tina used real examples from
Natalia's work, ensuring that the feedback was specific,
relevant, and actionable.

Outcome: Growth and Success

Over time, Natalia's performance significantly improved. She
became adept at managing complex client relationships, her
reports were consistently accurate, and she could handle
difficult client conversations with greater confidence. The
regular face-to-face interactions with Tina allowed for
immediate feedback and adjustments, accelerating Natalia's
learning curve.

Conclusion: Reflecting on the Journey

As their formal mentorship program neared its end, Tina and
Natalia reflected on their journey. They acknowledged the
challenges they overcame and celebrated Natalia's growth.
Tina expressed her belief in Natalia's abilities and uture in the
company, reinforcing the positive impact of their mentorship.
They agreed to continue their relationship informally, with
Tina available for guidance as Natalia progressed in her
career.

This case study demonstrates how active listening,
constructive feedback, handling difficult conversations, and
leveraging technology can play pivotal roles in a successful
face-to-face mentorship, leading to significant professional
growth for the mentee.

Case Study #2 – Remote, Business Development Case Study
Mentor: Ellie C.
Mentee: Veronica T.

Background
In the dynamic field of business development, a leading digital marketing agency, "Clicks and Giggles Digital Marketing," embraced remote work and mentorship. Ellie C., a veteran Business Development Director with extensive industry experience, was paired with Veronica T., an ambitious and talented junior business development executive who had recently joined the agency.

Setting the Stage: Embracing Remote Interaction
Ellie and Veronica's mentorship journey began with a virtual kick-off meeting. Utilizing Zoom for their face-to-face interactions, Ellie established the tone for open communication and trust. She engaged in active listening as Veronica shared her career goals, current skills, and the areas she felt needed improvement.

Leveraging Digital Tools
Recognizing the potential of technology in remote mentorship, Ellie introduced various digital platforms to streamline their interactions. They used Asana to set goals, tracking Veronica's progress, and scheduling their bi-weekly meetings. Additionally, Ellie showed Veronica how to use advanced client management software and analytics tools, vital in business development roles.

Navigating Challenges: Handling Difficult Conversations
Several months into the mentorship, Ellie observed a pattern in Veronica's client proposals; they were often overly ambitious, leading to unrealistic client expectations. Ellie initiated a difficult conversation during one of their video calls. She began by acknowledging Veronica's creativity and effort but then carefully pointed out the risks associated with

over-promising clients. She used specific examples from her proposals to illustrate her point.

Veronica, initially defensive, gradually opened up about her eagerness to impress clients and her fear of under-performing. Ellie's patient and understanding approach allowed Ellie to express her concerns openly and be receptive to her guidance.

Providing Constructive Feedback
Ellie offered Veronica constructive feedback. She praised her innovative ideas and strong client engagement skills but advised her to be more realistic and client-focused in her proposals. Ellie emphasized the importance of balancing creativity with practicality in business development.

Positive Outcome: Growth and Achievement
As the mentorship progressed, Veronica's skills in crafting balanced client proposals improved markedly. Her ability to set realistic project goals and manage client expectations evolved, leading to increased client satisfaction and fewer escalated issues. The remote nature of their mentorship did not hinder communication; instead, the digital tools facilitated a continuous and effective feedback loop.

Reflecting on the Mentorship Journey
After the formal mentorship program, Ellie and Veronica reviewed their journey. They acknowledged the initial challenges of remote communication and celebrated Veronica's professional growth. Ellie expressed her confidence in Veronica's future contributions to the agency and offered ongoing support as she advanced in her career.

This case study exemplifies how active listening, constructive feedback, handling difficult conversations, and effectively leveraging technology are crucial in a successful remote mentorship, particularly in the fast-paced world of business development. Ellie and Veronica's journey highlights the potential for significant growth and development, even when mentor and mentee are not physically co-located.

In conclusion, in Chapter 5 we learned that effective communication is the backbone of Mentorship Mastery. By actively listening, providing constructive feedback, navigating difficult conversations with finesse, and leveraging technology for remote mentorship, mentors and mentees can cultivate a communication-rich environment that propels them toward mutual success and growth.

List of Chapter 5 Highpoints:

- Active listening in mentorship fosters mutual understanding and respect and ensures that both parties feel heard and valued.
- Feedback that is honest and helpful, focuses on improvement and growth rather than criticism.
- Approaching and navigating difficult conversations, including dealing with disagreements, sensitive topics, and providing tough feedback can be challenging, requiring patience, open communication, and trust.
- In remote mentorship relationships, leveraging technology is essential to maintain effective communication and connection from a distance.
- To ensure a more effective mentorship experience, understanding and adapting to different communication styles must in in the toolbox of the mentor and mentee, because mentorship is a two-way process.

Call to Action for the Mentor:

1. In your next meeting, focus on actively listening to your mentee. This includes summarizing their points, asking clarifying questions, and avoiding interruption.
2. Use a method for feedback that is agreeable to the mentee that is constructive and positive. Avoid the "sandwich" method of feedback.

3. Plan and practice how you will approach challenging topics or feedback sessions to ensure they are constructive and empathetic.
4. Familiarize yourself with various digital communication tools and platforms to effectively connect with your mentee remotely.
5. Be aware of and adjust your communication style to match your mentee's preferences, whether they respond better to directness, storytelling, visual aids, or other methods.

Call to Action for the Mentee:

1. During discussions, actively engage by asking questions, expressing your thoughts, and summarizing key points to demonstrate understanding.
2. Approach feedback with an open mind. View it as an opportunity for growth and ask questions if you need more clarification.
3. If there is a topic you find challenging or uncomfortable, take the initiative to bring it up. Practice how you will present your concerns or questions.
4. Proactively use technology to stay in touch with your mentor. This can include regular emails, messages, or video calls. Discuss with them their preferred frequency, method, and technology.
5. Clearly communicate your needs, learning style, and any concerns to your mentor. This helps them tailor their mentoring approach to suit your best.

I. Conclusion

Mentorship, as presented in "Mentorship Mastery: Nurturing Growth and Success," is a dynamic and impactful journey that requires dedication, understanding, and adaptability from both mentors and mentees. By embracing the principles of empathy, clear communication, goal-setting, and effective matching, mentors, and mentees can cultivate relationships that not only foster individual growth but also contribute to the development of a nurturing and productive organization. This book serves as a guide to mastering the art of mentorship, with the aim of nurturing growth and success in various professional and personal facets of life. As we conclude, remember that the essence of mentorship lies in the mutual journey of learning, growing, and achieving together.

The power of mentorship lies in its ability to transform lives and careers, to forge powerful and supportive relationships, and to create a ripple effect of growth and learning that extends beyond the mentor-mentee duo. It is a testament to the fact that the journey of growth is often best navigated with the support and wisdom of someone who has walked the path before.

Please consider taking action to share your thoughts and experiences in mentorship. We welcome your real-world examples and will try to include them in our next book. While your experience is fresh on your mind, provide a review immediately on Amazon! I appreciate any feedback provided and it will be used to improve our book offerings for you and other readers.

Coming soon – "Mentorship Mastery: Sustaining Mentorships for the Long Haul"

II. Appendices

A. Mentorship Resources and Tools

https://nationalmentoringresourcecenter.org/resources-for-mentoring-programs/

https://ima.memberclicks.net/

B. Sample Mentorship Agreement (see below)

Mentorship Agreement

Mentor: [Mentor's Full Name] Mentee: [Mentee's Full Name] Date: [Date of Agreement]

Purpose:

This agreement outlines the framework for the mentorship relationship between [Mentor's Full Name] and [Mentee's Full Name]. It is intended to clarify the expectations and responsibilities of each party to ensure a productive and mutually beneficial relationship.

Goals and Objectives:

- **Mentee's Goals:** [List specific goals the mentee aims to achieve through this mentorship.]
- **Mentor's Role:** [Describe the mentor's role in supporting the mentee's goals, such as providing guidance, resources, etc.]

Commitment:

- **Duration of Mentorship:** [Specify the period for the mentorship, e.g., 6 months, 1 year, etc.]
- **Meeting Frequency and Format:** [Detail the agreed-upon frequency and format of meetings, e.g., once a month, in-person or virtual, etc.]
- **Availability:** [Outline expectations for availability and communication outside of scheduled meetings.]

Preferred Communication
- Mentee's Preferred Communication [Describe the mentee's preferred communication tools and technology.]
- Mentor's Preferred Communication [Describe the mentor's preferred communication tools and technology.]

Responsibilities:
- **Mentor Responsibilities:** [List responsibilities of the mentor, such as providing honest feedback, maintaining confidentiality, etc.]
- **Mentee Responsibilities:** [List responsibilities of the mentee, such as being initiative-taking in their development, preparing for meetings, etc.]

Confidentiality:
Both parties agree to maintain the confidentiality of the information shared in mentorship sessions unless mutually agreed upon or required by law.

Feedback and Evaluation:
Both mentor and mentee agree to provide regular feedback to each other and to evaluate the progress of the mentorship relationship at regular intervals.

Adaptability and Changes:
Both parties agree to be open to adjusting this agreement as needed to reflect changes in goals, availability, or other circumstances.

Termination of Mentorship:
Either party may decide to terminate the mentorship relationship at any point. In such a case, a final meeting is encouraged to provide closure and to reflect on the learning and growth experienced during the mentorship.

Signatures:
By signing below, both parties agree to the terms of

this mentorship agreement and commit to working collaboratively towards the achievement of the outlined goals.

Mentor Signature:_________________**Date:** _________

Mentee Signature: _______________**Date:** ________

Note: This agreement is a guiding document and is not legally binding. It serves to clarify and set expectations for the mentorship relationship.

III. Terms and Definitions

Alumni Network – refers to the collective and interconnected nature of past participants in a mentorship program.

Champion – A champion in a workplace or organizational setting is someone who actively and enthusiastically supports, advocates for, and promotes an individual, a project, or a cause. A champion's primary function is advocacy and promotion.

Coaching – Coaching is a structured, goal-focused process led by a coach who employs specific techniques and methodologies to enhance an individual's abilities, knowledge, or performance in specific areas. Coaching is particularly effective in environments where specific skill acquisition or performance improvement is needed in a brief period.

Diversity – Refers to the inclusion and representation of a wide range of characteristics and attributes in a mentorship program or relationship. This can encompass, but is not limited to, differences in race, ethnicity, gender, sexual orientation, age, physical abilities, religious beliefs, socioeconomic status, experiences, and perspectives. In mentorship diversity plays several crucial roles:
- Broadening Perspectives
- Enhancing Learning
- Fostering Innovation
- Building Empathy and Cultural Confidence
- Promotion Equity and Inclusion
- Career Advancement

Emotional Intelligence – In the context of mentorship, emotional intelligence (EI) refers to the mentor's ability to understand, manage, and effectively express their own emotions, as well as to interpret and respond appropriately to

the emotions of their mentee. Key aspects of EI in mentorship
include:

- Self-Awareness
- Self-Regulation
- Motivation
- Empathy
- Social Skills

Empathy – Refers to the mentor/mentee's ability to
understand, share, and genuinely relate to the feelings,
thoughts, and experiences of each other. It involves a deep
level of emotional and cognitive awareness where the
mentor/mentee can put themselves in the other's shoes,
appreciate their perspective, and respond with sensitivity and
understanding. Empathy in mentorship plays several critical
roles:

- Building Trust and Rapport
- Enhanced Understanding
- Effective Communication
- Supportive Environment
- Personalized Guidance
- Conflict Resolution
- Emotional Support

Equity – Refers to the practice of ensuring fair and impartial
treatment, access, opportunity, and advancement for all
mentees, while striving to identify and eliminate barriers that
have prevented the full participation of some individuals or
groups. Equity in mentorship involves recognizing and
addressing disparities within the mentoring environment and
tailoring support to meet the unique needs and circumstances
of each mentee. Key aspects of equity in mentorship include:

- Individualized Support
- Accessibility
- Inclusive Practices
- Addressing Systemic Barriers
- Cultivating a Diverse Mentor Pool
- Promotion Fair Opportunities

External Mentorship – Is a structured relationship in which an individual seeking guidance and support, receives mentorship and advice from an experienced and knowledgeable individual who is outside their immediate organization or professional network. In external mentorship, the mentor typically possesses expertise and insights in areas relevant to the mentee's personal or professional development goals.

Formal Mentorship – A formal mentorship opportunity is a structured and organized program designed to facilitate mentor-mentee relationships. Unlike informal mentorship, which develops naturally, formal mentorship is typically initiated and supported by an organization or a specific program with defined objectives and guidelines. Key characteristics of formal mentorship include:
- Structured Matching
- Clear Objectives
- Scheduled Meetings
- During
- Training and Resources
- Monitoring & Support
- Formal Recognition

Imposter Syndrome – Also known as imposter phenomenon, refers to a psychological pattern where individuals, despite external evidence of their competence and accomplishments, believe they do not deserve their success. They often fear being exposed as a "fraud" and attribute their achievements to luck or external factors rather than their abilities.

Inclusion – Refers to the practice of creating an environment where all individuals, regardless of their diverse backgrounds, characteristics, and experiences, feel valued, respected, and supported. It involves ensuring that everyone has equal access to mentorship opportunities and that these experiences are welcoming and accommodating to people from all levels of society. In a mentorship setting, inclusion encompasses several key aspects:
- Welcoming Diversity

- Equal Opportunity and Access
- Tailored Support
- Encouraging Diverse Perspectives
- Creating a Safe and Open Environment
- Cultural Sensitivity
- Inclusive Communication

Informal Mentorship – An informal mentorship opportunity is a type of mentorship that occurs organically, without a structured or formalized program. It usually develops naturally based on mutual interests, shared professional goals, or compatible personalities. Characteristics include:

- Flexibility
- Personal Connection
- Organic Development
- Adaptive Goals
- No Formal Timeframe

Internal Mentorship – Often referred to as "organizational mentorship," is a structured and intentional mentoring relationship that occurs within an organization or company. In internal mentorship, an experienced and knowledgeable employee, known as the mentor, provides guidance, support, and knowledge transfer to a less-experienced colleague or mentee within the same organization.

Mentorship – Mentorship is a developmental relationship where a more experienced or knowledgeable person (the mentor) guides a less experienced or knowledgeable person (the mentee) through personal and professional growth. It is characterized as a longer-term relationship that focuses on the overall development of the mentee.

Organizational Mentorship – See *"Internal Mentorship"*

Peer Mentoring – Peer Mentoring is a type of mentorship where individuals at similar career stages or with similar levels of experience guide and support each other. Unlike traditional mentorship, which often involves a more experienced individual mentoring a less experienced one, peer

mentoring is based on the principle of mutual learning and
growth. Key aspects of Peer Mentoring include:

- Shared Learning
- Mutual Support
- Collaborative Problem Solving
- Networking and Relationship Building
- Informal Nature

Reflection - "Reflection" in mentorship is practiced by both
mentor and mentee and refers to the process of thoughtfully
considering one's experiences, actions, feelings, and responses
to gain a deeper understanding of oneself and one's
professional journey. It involves critically examining both
successes and challenges to extract valuable lessons and
insights.

Scenario Analysis - Is a strategic planning method used to
make flexible long-term plans. It is a process of analyzing
future events by considering alternative outcomes (scenarios).
The method is used for risk management and long-term
planning.

Skills Gap Analysis – A skills gap analysis is a method used
by organizations to identify the differences between the skills
that are required for a job or within a workforce and the actual
skills that employees possess. It is a systematic process that
helps to pinpoint specific areas where employees' skills and
knowledge may not align with the company's goals,
performance expectations, or industry standards. The steps
involved include:

- Identifying Required Skills
- Assessing Current Skills
- Analyzing the Gap
- Developing Strategies to Bridge the Gap
- Implementing Solutions and Monitoring Progress

Soft Skills – Refers to the non-technical, interpersonal
attributes and personal traits that determine how individuals
interact effectively and harmoniously with others. These skills
are crucial for both mentors and mentees, as they significantly

influence the dynamics of the mentorship relationship and its overall effectiveness. Key soft skills in mentorship include:
- Communication Skills
- Empathy
- Emotional Intelligence
- People Skills
- Conflict Resolution
- Adaptability and Flexibility

IV. References

[1] Together Mentorship Software. (n.d.).
https://www.togetherplatform.com/case-studies/cooley

[2] Chellappa, S. (2023, September 14). 5 Coaching and mentoring examples to empower workplaces. Engagedly.
https://engagedly.com/blog/inspiring-examples-of-coaching-and-mentoring-in-the-workplace/

[3] Shawn Branchard, "Three Phases of Mentorship" TEDMUSKEGON presentation. (2016)

[4] What mentorship Really Means, Simon Sinek, Book Club with Simon, May 2020

[5] The Mutual Benefits of Mentorship | Vinnie Malcolm | TEDxManhattanBeach (youtube.com) (March 2022)

[6] Clance, P. and Imes, S., "The Impostor Phenomenon in High Achieving Women: Dynamics and Therapeutic Intervention." (1978)

[7] McCarthy Mentoring. (2020, January 23). Why mentoring: what the stats say. McCarthy Mentoring | Inspiring Leaders.
https://mccarthymentoring.com/why-mentoring-what-the-stats-say/

[8] Kristine Zedek, (14) Post | LinkedIn, (2023)

[9] Zinnov. (2019). Why Corporate Mentorship Programs Are Key To Innovation.

[10] Anderson, G. O. (2019, January). Mentorship and the Value of a Multigenerational Workforce. AARP.
https://doi.org/10.26419/res.00270.001

[11] Toke, N., Toke, N., Toke, N., & Toke, N. (2023, July 10). Embracing Multigenerational workforce and Diversity in the workplace [2024 DEI Resources] | Diversity for Social Impact. Diversity for Social ImpactTM. https://diversity.social/embracing-multigenerational-workforce/

[12] https://crucial learning.com/browse-courses/crucial-conversations-fordialogue/

[13] Blanchard, K. H., & Johnson, S. (1982). The one minute manager. https://cqx.sagepub.com/content/23/4/39.full.pdf

[14] Stone, D. M., & Heen, S. (2014). Thanks for the feedback: the science and art of receiving feedback well. https://openlibrary.org/books/OL27557979M/Thanks_for_the_Feedback

[15] Engel. (1988). The Socratic Method. Routledge.